"There is no space here to indicate how incisively and vividly, with what fullness of reference to history, Scripture and current theology Fr. Godfrey writes, or how many fresh vistas he has opened to his audience . . . One can wish for this book only the widest possible circulation and the deepest pondering."   *America*

"This book has been given much deserved praise. It is concerned with a facet of Christian life very much to the fore at present—the liturgy. In style the book is lively, crisp, popular, and contains solid history, theology, and pastoral concern."   *Cross and Crown*

"The fact that the liturgical movement in America has remained on solid theological ground is due, in great part, to Father Diekmann's sound insight and practical concern for its continued advancement."   *Ave Maria*

"This is liturgical writing at its best, Fr. Diekmann's chapters on the sacraments are especially valuable and reveal the sound theological basis of the liturgical movement. This book is another fine addition to the liturgical library."   *The Way*

"Many striking insights can be found here as to the inner meaning of the liturgy, and its application to the search for holiness in this modern day."   *The Liguorian*

"Father Diekmann covers the whole life of worship from sacramentals to the exalted place of the bishop in the liturgy. He has deep theological insights into our relationship with Christ through the Mass and the sacraments."   *The Sign*

"Superb treatise on the Mass and the sacraments and our whole liturgical life."   *Catholic Bulletin*

COME, LET US WORSHIP

GODFREY DIEKMANN, O.S.B.

WITH A NEW INTRODUCTION

IMAGE BOOKS

A DIVISION OF DOUBLEDAY & COMPANY, INC.

GARDEN CITY, NEW YORK

Image Books Edition: 1966
by special arrangement with Helicon Press, Inc.
Image Books Edition published September, 1966

Nihil Obstat: EDWARD A. CERNY, S.S., S.T.D.
    Censor Librorum

Imprimatur: ✠ FRANCIS P. KEOUGH, D.D.
    Archbishop of Baltimore
    June 26, 1961

The Nihil Obstat and Imprimatur are official declarations that a
book or pamphlet is free of doctrinal or moral error. No
implication is contained therein that those who have granted
the Nihil Obstat and Imprimatur agree with the opinions
expressed.

This volume is the second in a series entitled Benedictine Studies
sponsored by The American Benedictine Academy and published by Helicon Press, Inc., Baltimore, Md. 21202.

Helicon Press gratefully acknowledges the kind permission of the
Liturgical Conference to reprint those portions of this book
which were originally presented as addresses at Liturgical Weeks
in recent years. The places and dates of these Liturgical Weeks
are indicated on the first page of each chapter.

INTRODUCTION

When, contrary to earlier announced plans, the schema on the liturgy was presented to the Council Fathers as the first matter for discussion in the fall of 1962, the news came as a surprise and disappointment to many. Criticism became more pronounced when the major part of the Council's first session was taken up with seemingly insignificant argumentation about liturgical reforms. Why waste precious time on such trivia, when the vast task of the Church's renewal was the proclaimed aim of the Council, and there were so many other documents of obviously more serious import that demanded attention?

Now, four years later, the Council has completed its work, and it is generally conceded by both Catholics and non-Catholics that giving priority to the liturgy schema was a happy decision. Several of the Protestant Observers at the Council, indeed, have publicly stated their conviction that even if the Council had accomplished nothing else, the promulgation of the Liturgy Constitution would have sufficed to rank it among the most important councils of Christian history.

Precisely because Vatican Council II was dedicated to the renewal of the Church, the reform and promotion of the liturgy deserved priority: for, "the liturgy, 'through which the work of our redemption is accomplished,' most of all in the divine sacrifice of the Eucharist, is the outstanding means whereby the faithful may express in their lives, and manifest to others, the mystery of Christ and the real nature of the true Church" (Art. 2). The Church is the people of God whose first and most important duty and privilege it is to worship Him; and it is in that worship that they are to discover and embrace the true dimensions of their Christian apostolate in the world. "The liturgy is the summit towards which the activity of the Church is directed; at the same time it is fount from which all her power flows" (Art. 10). Hence the imperative need of reforming the liturgy so that participation in it will indeed be "active, intelligent, *and easy.*"

It seems likely, however, that the decisive reason motivating the choice of the liturgy schema as first on the agenda may not have been the above considerations, however logical they now appear, but the simple fact that more preparatory ground-work had evidently been done in the question of liturgy reform than in any of the other matters slated for discussion. Moreover, the acknowledged pastoral scope of the liturgy recommended itself to a Council whose professed aim was pastoral renewal. The liturgical movement had a grass-roots history of forty years; and papal encouragement and sanction had been added by Pope Pius XII's encyclical *Mediator Dei* in 1947, as well as by the *Instruction* of 1958. International liturgical study weeks had also contributed to effect a substantial agreement among liturgical leaders as to the nature and relative urgency of future reforms. And it was from among these leaders that the preparatory commission responsible for drafting the liturgy schema was largely chosen.

Most significantly of all, their substantial consensus derived from the pastoral experiences of some four decades of the liturgical movement in all parts of the Catholic world. It was by actually praying and singing together in eucharistic worship above all, that the faithful had become more clearly aware once again that they *are* the Church; that "we, though many, are one body, because we partake of the one bread"—and therefore must manifest this unity in daily concern for our fellow-man; that all present have a distinctive and divinely willed office to perform in the communal action, that of the ordained priest being the office of ministry; that Christ is present not only under the eucharistic species, but that He is present as the head to his body in the midst of this specific worshiping assembly, and more particularly when He addresses them through the proclaimed Scriptures; that it is the communal *"celebration"* which most effectively stirs and nourishes the faith which is the measure of our sharing in the paschal mysteries.

In a word, the experience of the liturgical movement had brought with it a new and invigorating self-awareness on the part of the Church. This then found formulation in the Constitution on the Sacred Liturgy—and was reflected in the subsequent documents. The Church had freshly experienced herself in that eucharistic Action which the Council declares to be her most important manifestation or self-realization. It is the living Church, actively engaged "in the same Eucharist, in a single prayer, at one altar, at which presides the bishop surrounded by his college of priests and by his ministers" (Art. 41), which to a remarkable degree determined the ecclesiological pronouncements of the Council.

But though the Church had experienced herself in liturgical celebrations, it was this same pastoral experience, too, which had shown how these celebrations could and should be reformed in order to manifest the true nature of the Church more clearly and convincingly. Since the sacraments, including the Eucharist, are "signs of faith," the signs had to be made more easily intelligible. Such had been the insistent plea of the liturgists. The Council responded with a thoroughness which surpassed all previous hope. Some changes have already been introduced; but the effective implementation of the Council's principles of liturgical reform is the task of the post-conciliar Concilium appointed for this purpose, whose members are presently devoting energetic efforts to its accomplishment. Because of the critical importance of their work for the well-being of the entire Church, our prayer should support their labors.

Several commentaries on the Liturgy Constitution have already appeared, and still more are needed to achieve knowledgeable collaboration of priests and faithful in the Council's program of renewal. It may therefore be fairly asked: Why bother to reprint essays on the liturgy some of which antedate the Council by many years?

A partial answer is already implicit in the foregoing. The Council's constitution on the liturgy, to a greater extent than any of its other documents, is the precipitate of many years of pastoral experience and related theorizing. The reforms now ordered are for the most part those for which two generations of liturgical writers had agitated, and the doctrinal context of the Constitution sanctions the theological emphases which liturgists had long been urging. There is striking continuity, though of course not identity, between the Constitution on the Sacred Liturgy and the agreed concerns of the liturgical movement that preceded it.

It would have been an easy matter to alter or bring up to date what I had written. I thought it preferable, however, to let the record stand. Its substance, I believe, is still sound. And it may prove interesting to note to what extent at least one proponent of the liturgical movement in America had succeeded or failed in witnessing to the developing spiritual current which has issued into the basic renewal document of Vatican Council II.

Godfrey Diekmann, O.S.B.
February 19, 1966

TABLE OF CONTENTS

COME, LET US WORSHIP

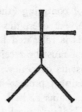

FOREWORD

"Tell me, Peter, what does it mean to you to be a disciple of Christ?"

When Father Godfrey Diekmann conducted the retreat exercises for the clergy of the State of Oregon, he speculated on the different answers that the Prince of the Apostles might have given to that question before and after the Last Supper.

Before he had listened to the last discourse of Christ, the good, gruff and child-like Peter might have informed his questioner that being a disciple meant most of all loyalty to the Master, imitation of His example and following Him, come what might.

But after the Last Supper, the apostle would have realized that there was far more to the message of Christ. In fact it is possible that he would have been so overwhelmed, so filled with gratitude and wonder at his dignity that he could not have spoken at all. For he could have realized for the first time what it really meant to be a disciple of Christ.

In this volume, Father Godfrey presents that full and vivid insight into the doctrines of faith that could cause our hearers to echo: "I never realized before what it really means to be a disciple of Christ!"

Unfortunately, for too many people, Christianity is not the glad tidings of salvation but merely a system of moralizing—a rigid collection of do's and don't's. Christian dogma for many is not a wonderfully unified framework but merely a list of disjointed articles that must be believed. The holy law of God is seen as merely a set of confining (though necessary) regulations that must be observed; even the life-giving contact with Christ in His sacraments is relegated by some to the status of little understood rites that must be received. For too many moderns, Christianity has lost its good news and has become a burden, a discouragingly painful process—the necessary minimum requirement to avoid the pains of hell.

That is why Father Godfrey's work comes as such a refreshing change: "Christianity is glad tidings; not a hard bargain that God drives with man. We are not mere creatures, doing our best, and hoping for future union with God as a reward. Christianity is not just a ladder that we must climb by our good works in order finally to achieve heaven. By the sacraments, we are already on the divine level, we are sons of God, citizens of heaven. And all our moral effort now consists in putting away the human hindrances that prevent the divine life from flowering in us.

"Morality does not mean becoming something, so much as being something. Be yourself. Act your age. Or, more elegantly, in the words of St. Leo the Great: 'Christian, remember your dignity.' Walk worthy of the calling with which you have been called. Walk worthy of the sacraments by which Christ lives, and wishes to act, in you."

The moral life is presented by Father Godfrey as a "divine urgency" in us. It is not something that we can choose to follow at our own pace, while we manage to slip into heaven at the very last moment by an act of perfect contrition. It is "a life that demands growth, a divine urgency that may not be denied except at the risk of total loss."

Only to those who look to the liturgical movement for some spectacular or novel fadism will Father Godfrey's book prove a disappointment. His approach to Christianity is as old as St. Paul's—"proclaiming the mystery of Christ." For him, the touchstone of Christian piety is still the answer to the question first posed to the Apostles: "What think you of Christ?" His treatment of sacramental theology is a carefully documented "rediscovery" of St. Thomas. He uses the most authoritative sources of Christian tradition to sketch the role of priest and people at Holy Mass. In discussing such topics as the church year, faith, or devotion to the Blessed Mother, he relies heavily on the patristic writings.

The editor of *Worship* brings to his task a profound grasp of dogma and sacred scripture and exhibits a truly remarkable working knowledge of the fathers of the Church. His volume bespeaks the maturity achieved by the liturgical renewal in the United States: its foundations solidly based on theology and scripture, yet deeply in sympathy with the task of catechetics and the practical problems of pastoral life.

It seems especially providential that the twentieth century should see the rapid and simultaneous growth of three great revivals within the Church—liturgical, biblical and catechetical. It is but natural that a renewed liturgical fervor should bring about a greater love for the holy bible. Pope John XXIII told groups of pilgrims about the two prized treasures of our faith: the book and the cup—the bible and the Eucharist. If we grow in appreciation for the Word of God as written in the bible and as embodied in the liturgy, we must of necessity deepen our zeal to proclaim that Word to the world. This is the catechetical movement.

It is especially heartening that these great modern stirrings of the Spirit in the Church have American spokesmen as competent as Godfrey Diekmann, O.S.B. In his papers to the National Liturgical Weeks (which are reprinted in this book), in the monthly review which he edits, as well as in his retreat conferences to our clergy, we have found his presentation solidly theological yet eminently practical.

Volumes such as this should go a long way toward clearing any misconceptions or lack of understanding that might still exist concerning the nature or true goals of the liturgical apostolate. It has been said that in the pioneer days, popular sentiment thought that the liturgical apostolate had something to do with trimming lace off albs or sawing backs off altars. Later many supposed that the ultimate aim of the so-called "liturgists" was to have vocal participation in the recited or sung Mass. It has been only recently, so the story goes, that the liturgical movement has been able to communicate to the great body of the faithful that the primary aim of this apostolate is to make people holy, to conform them to Christ.

Our country does not seem to be alone in this problem. In his Lenten Pastoral of 1958, Pope Paul VI, then Cardinal Montini, told the faithful of Milan that there are still those who consider the liturgical renewal as "an optional matter, or as one of the numerous devotional currents to which a person may adhere or not, as he chooses." He regretted that the mentality still exists "which thinks that the liturgical movement is a troublesome attempt at reformation, of doubtful orthodoxy, or a petrified, external ritualism which has to do merely with rubrics, or an archeological fad, formalistic and 'arty,' or else a product of the cloister ill adapted to the people of our world, or a preconceived opposition to personal piety and popular devotions."

In season and out of season we must remind our people that the purpose of the liturgical apostolate is to draw them closer to the heavenly Father in union with Christ. The liturgy is the Church's official school of holiness; in fact it is the only system of spirituality made of obligation by Mother Church. Pope Pius XII called the liturgy the most effective means of achieving holiness. We read in *Mediator Dei:* "It should be clear to all then, that the worship rendered to God by the Church in union with her divine head is the most efficacious means of achieving sanctity."

Commenting on this passage from the encyclical, Cardinal Montini, writes in the 1958 Pastoral: "Hence we must welcome the liturgical renewal as the means of the religious rebirth and the form which that rebirth must take, according to the spirit and laws of Mother Church." While still serving in the Vatican Secretariate, Monsignor Montini wrote to the Liturgical Week in Oropa: "Nothing is more urgent in this hour, so grave and yet so rich in hopes, than to call the people of God, the great family of Jesus Christ, back to the substantial food of liturgical piety, revived by the breath of the Holy Spirit, who is the soul of the Church and of each one of her children."

Every pastor of souls can agree from bitter experience that the revival of the Christian spirit is the most urgent problem of our times. Around us we see a rising tide of lawlessness and godlessness; we live in a culture dedicated to fun, worldly security, and creature comfort. Still it is useless to decry the secularization of society and the decline of morality unless we are prepared with positive steps to bring men into contact with the spirit of Christ. Where else can our world re-learn the true Christian spirit if not from the liturgy—"that primary and indispensable source?"

The reasons that Cardinal Montini lists for a liturgical revival are as compelling for America as they are for the Archdiocese of Milan:

The spiritual decadence of our times demands it.
The cultural development of our people demands it.
The inner vitality of holy Church demands it.
The teaching authority of the Church demands it.
The eternal bidding of Christ: 'Do this in memory of me,' demands it.

To these cogent reasons, we add the clear summons of Pope Pius XII: "The faithful should be aware that to participate in the eucharistic sacrifice is their chief duty and their supreme dignity."

Since the liturgical movement is of such vital importance, we can be truly thankful to divine providence for giving America pioneers who have been so foresighted and yet remarkably prudent. Though we could not presume to name them all, we must pay a well-deserved tribute to such outstanding figures as Archbishop Edwin V. O'Hara, Father Virgil Michel, O.S.B., Father H. A. Reinhold, Father Mathis, C.S.C., as well as the Benedictine scholar who penned this book.

This is a book that the priest would do well to bring to his predieu and the seminarian to his prayer hall. Father Godfrey's volume affords that insight into the Christian faith that a bishop would pray to find in his deacons on ordination day. We know of no higher tribute to pay it.

✠ Edward D. Howard
Archbishop of Portland in Oregon

3 May 1961

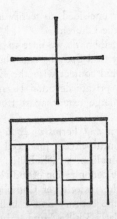

PART ONE

POPULAR PARTICIPATION AND THE HISTORY
OF CHRISTIAN PIETY

It would seem high time that we stop blaming the Protestant Reformation, or, if you wish, Catholic polemic reaction to it, for all the spiritual ills we find ourselves heir to. Protestantism has all too long served as a convenient scapegoat, for instance, for explaining how it happened that the doctrine of the Mystical Body, or lay participation in the Mass, suffered eclipse, or that there developed a practical divorce between the sacraments and personal piety.

Obviously Protestantism, and reaction to it, hardened in some instances an undesirable status quo. Thus, to quote but evident instances: Protestant rejection of the hierarchical Church, and Protestant exaggeration of the priesthood of the laity postponed for centuries a more balanced presentation of the Mystical Body and all that this doctrine involves in such activities as the lay apostolate and participation in the liturgy. But we should not lose sight of the fact that in these matters the Protestant revolt was itself an effort, however one-sided, to rectify an imbalance that existed at the time in the Church.

How far back into history, then, do we have to go to discover when the doctrine of the Mystical Body became obscured; when the laity lost living, devotional contact with the Eucharist and the other sacraments; when private devotion began to develop parallel to, and then to a large extent apart from, its sacramental sources?

Louis Bouyer, in his *Spirit and Forms of Protestantism*, has called attention to the harmful effects produced by Ockham and his philosophy of nominalism, which by its contempt of universals might be called the canonization of individualism, and which was triumphant in the majority of Catholic theological faculties in universities in the century and a half which preceded Luther's revolt. Similarly Philip Hughes has passed severe strictures (in vol. 3 of his *History of the Church*) on the *Devotio Moderna*, which, according to him, was too largely a religious subjectivism, suspicious of theological learning, and proved, despite its undoubted positive merits, a fatally inadequate bulwark against the Protestant flood.

But subjectivism and individualism, unthinkable if the doctrine of the Mystical Body had been to the forefront of Christian thinking, were themselves but symptoms of a spiritual malaise which had its causes in developments centuries earlier.

How early?. It is impossible of course to suggest a definite date, e.g., A.D. 800. Movements of the spirit, of culture and thought, do not begin at twelve o'clock midnight of a given day and year. But evidently it can be stated with certainty, as a result of modern research, that the doctrine of the Mystical Body became obscured in the five centuries that intervened between the era of the Fathers (ending with Gregory the Great, about A.D. 600) and the beginnings of scholasticism. In other words, between 600 and 1100. And the obscuring of this doctrine brought with it the eclipse, partial, and often seemingly total, in the consciousness of the faithful of many related consequences, including the role of the laity in respect to the Eucharist and sacraments, and in the life of the Church generally.

This discovery is, as just indicated, a relatively recent one. A current standard reference has been, for instance, the four-volume work of Pourrat on *Christian Spirituality*. Now it is significant that Pourrat devotes the first volume to the era of the Fathers, i.e., to the first 600 years; then he begins the second volume (after a short, five-page nod to Cluny) with Saint Bernard, five centuries after the era of the Fathers, thus covering these five centuries in five pages! And yet in the 2000 years of the Church's existence, there has never been a more momentous change of outlook and practice in Christian spirituality than in these five centuries. Fortunately, the projected new history of spirituality now being prepared by Père Bouyer, Dom Leclercq, Dom Vandenbroucke and others, promises to do greater justice to this neglected period.

Though it would be easy to present in detail a contrast between participation of the laity in the patristic era and five hundred years later, a few examples may suffice:

In the earlier centuries the people answered their "Amens" to the prayers of the priest, and especially to the great Eucharistic prayer, which was recited aloud in a language they understood. The bond between altar and congregation was intimate, constantly renewed by the dialogue between celebrant and people. And it was taken for granted that reception of Holy Communion was the normal conclusion of the Eucharistic service. And by 1100? The contrast could hardly be more drastic. The Mass had become almost exclusively a priestly activity and service. At the canon the priest, like Moses, climbed the sacred mountain alone and the people were left behind at the foot of the mountain, at best engaged in prayerful meditation on the events of Christ's life on the basis of an artificial, allegorical interpretation of some of the visible, external rites. The inner meaning of the heart of the Mass was shut to them. The Eucharistic prayer was recited by the priest in silence; the Mass of the Catechumens was in a language not understood by them; and Holy Communion itself had become a rare event, reserved for some of the great feastdays.

Why this change? Various explanations have been proposed, and probably all to a certain extent supplement one another. It seems that ultimately the solution is to be sought in the answer given to the query, "What think ye of Christ?" That question with its answer was and always will be the touchstone of Christian thought and piety.

The greatest of all the ancient heresies was Arianism, which denied the divinity of Christ. The struggle with Arianism took place chiefly in the East. The West at that time remained relatively unscathed, particularly because of the clarity of the Latin terminology given to the Western Church by Tertullian. But the West also suffered and suffered severely with the coming of the barbarian tribes. The Visigoths had become Arians already under Emperor Valens in the fourth century in the East. And they infected their related tribes. When these tribes flooded over the West, particularly in the fifth century, practically all of them were, not heathens, but Arians or semi-Arians, and they dominated North Italy, South France, North Africa and, above all, Spain. Spain was the main battlefield. In Spain the anti-Arian struggle reached its height in the sixth century. And in Spain, as a consequence, the main trends of the reaction to Arianism developed most clearly and most vigorously. The flourishing Church in Spain in the seventh century then became, with its anti-Arian orientation, a model for other parts of the West, especially the Irish and English peoples. From Ireland and England, this specific theological, liturgical and spiritual climate was brought to France, particularly through the Irish monks, and through Alcuin at the court of Charlemagne. Finally, aided by the political supremacy in Italy of the Ottonian emperors, this Frankish or Nordic spiritual outlook made its influence felt in Rome itself.

More specifically, what were the long-range effects of this anti-Arian struggle? Arianism, as stated, denied the divinity of Christ. In reaction to it, there was an emphasis, a one-sided emphasis, on the divinity of Christ. It should be kept clearly in mind that this one-sided emphasis was not a question of orthodoxy, but rather of seeing certain truths out of focus: just as in a picture from a camera sharply focused on a specific object, the neighboring objects are often very blurred. Now what were the effects, the long-range effects?

First of all, in regard to the Eucharist. If Christ is regarded too one-sidedly in His divinity, we are apt to forget that He did not come on earth primarily to be worshipped, but to place Himself at the head of a redeemed humanity, leading them in worshipful submission back to the Father as His adopted sons. However much Christ deserves to be Himself worshipped—and He was worshipped from the earliest centuries of the Church—in His task as *Redeemer* (and that is what is re-enacted in holy Mass) He stands on the side of *humanity*, serving us; as He himself stated, precisely at the Last Supper: "I stand in the midst of you as one who serves."

But in the climate of the anti-Arian reaction, "Christ no longer stands by man's side as the representative and advocate of mankind; and He as the man, Christ Jesus, and the Firstborn of His brethren, no longer offers the sacrifice of mankind to the Triune God. He has, so to speak, crossed over, and is now on God's side, and Himself is the awful and unapproachable God" (Karl Adam, *Christ Our Brother*, p. 49). Deriving from this background we have the growing emphasis, even in the Mass prayers themselves, on the Trinity: prayers directed to the Trinity. The memory of the God-Man, who instituted the sacrifice, is overlaid by the thought of the divine Presence. Jesus is now the divine *Consecrator*.

I believe that this word is critical. Christ is viewed primarily as God, the divine Consecrator who effects the holy Sacrifice through His ministers, the priests. The faithful felt themselves faced by infinitely awful reality—the stupendous fact that God immolates Himself for man. In a word, holy Mass is no longer understood as a common action of the people of God, with and through their priests, with and through the Church, with and through their High Priest, the Man-God, Christ—but a service at which God becomes present in their midst, through the ministry of His priests. The Mass is *the action of God*. Christ is regarded not so much our High Priest as the divine Consecrator.

Here we have the theological thinking which brought with it an inevitable clericalization of the Mass: that is to say, the attitude that the priests alone, as the agents of God, have an active role in the stupendous miracle of the divine Presence on our altars. The principle of the distribution of roles—the principle that the priest has his part, the deacon and sub-deacon each his own, and the laity their rightful active role, which the

September 1958 Instruction of the Sacred Congregation of Rites makes so very clear—to all intents and purposes has disappeared. The canon of the Mass in which this miracle of divine Presence occurs has become the Holy of Holies, to which the ordained priest alone may have access. The Eucharistic prayer which the *Church* offers to the Father has become the *periculosa oratio*—the dangerous prayer, as some of the Celtic documents call it, and about whose recitation detailed warnings are laid down for the celebrant.

Inevitably, too, this novel view led to the *silent* canon, first introduced into France about the year 800. The people have no right, it was thought, to follow into the Holy of Holies! And to occupy them, Amalarius and his many imitators gave them those allegorical interpretations which dominated the field of the faithful's piety with certain ups and downs to our own day. True, no one dreamed of calling into question the theology of the Mass Sacrifice as formulated, for instance, later by the scholastics. But it simply did not penetrate into the popular explanations of the Mass. In these, the allegorical methods of Amalarius and his followers had undisputed monopoly. Even St. Thomas, in his treatment of the Mass in the *Summa*, was astonishingly influenced by them. And they are still with us!

That these and other popular Mass interpretations through the centuries since Amalarius had little meaningful relation to what the celebrant was actually reciting in the name of the community has been conclusively proved by the scholar André Wilmart in his essay, "Expositio Missae," in the *Dictionnaire d'Archéologie Chrétienne et de Liturgie*. The physical silence of the canon had become a blackout of prayerful comprehension.

This "clericalization" of the Mass led to the introduction into the Mass of private prayers of the priest, and led even, as we know, to a change in the text of the very canon. The original text of the first memento prayer in the canon had simply: *"Qui tibi offerunt sacrificium laudis"*: that is, "Remember Lord all here present who offer to Thee this sacrifice of praise." When the faithful no longer had an active part, this expression seemed too bold, and so the words *"pro quibus tibi offerimus*—for whom we, Thy ministers, offer" were introduced. This interpolation first appeared, significantly, about the year 800 in the Gregorian

Sacramentary prepared by Alcuin, and by the tenth century was quite universal.

To put it bluntly: the laity were in practice excluded from actual sharing in the heart of the Sacrifice, as soon as Christ's divinity was over-extolled at the expense of His high-priestly humanity.

This and this only seems an adequate explanation of what is now known as the vernacular problem. At the beginning of the third century the transition from Greek to Latin took place as a matter of course, without much argument, simply because Greek was no longer understood by the people. And no one questioned that the people had a right to understand, because holy Mass was the sacrificial worship, not only of *nos servi tui*, but also of *plebs tua sancta*—of Thy holy people. Five centuries later Latin was no longer understood except by the clergy and a few educated laymen. It may be true, as has been proposed, that Charlemagne strongly urged the retention of Latin as a unifying bond in his far-flung empire. It is true that the Romance languages had not yet developed into really suitable literary vehicles. But there was no similar outcry against barbaric tongues when Bishop Ulfilas, the Apostle of the Goths, in the fourth century translated the Scriptures into the Gothic tongue, which probably was a more crude vehicle of speech than the Romance languages of the eighth and ninth centuries. And Holy Scripture, when all is said and done, is a more direct and important expression of the word of God than any liturgical non-Biblical text.

The liturgy of the West was retained in Latin at this period of history, and no serious objection was raised, because it was no longer admitted nor understood, in circles high or low, that the people had a right to understand and to take part. A barrier had been erected between altar and nave that was never effectually removed until the 20th century, a barrier of which the roodscreen in later Gothic churches was only a logical external expression.

And yet the Eucharist, as it must at all times, remained central in Christian piety. Not the Eucharist as the communal action of priest and flock, but now the Eucharist as the Epiphany, the appearance of God among His people. The story of the wave of piety associated with the people's desire to see the Host, beginning in the 12th century, is a generally known fact of history. Authors have called it a Corpus Christi piety. In itself it was the strongest evidence of a predominantly subjective piety, divorced from the primary scope of the sacrifice-sacrament of the Eucharist. And history attests, too, what superstitious beliefs and practices were often bound up with it. There was true devotion, and very edifying worship of the Eucharist; but there was not that true eucharistic worship which, as the September 1958 Instruction tells us, the very nature of the Mass demands. Nobody except a few French theologians, therefore, seemed to find it strange when Pope Alexander VII in 1661 forbade the translation of the Mass prayers into the vernacular, a prohibition which was renewed as late as 1857 by Pope Pius IX, and tacitly dropped only under Pope Leo XIII in 1897.

As Father Jungmann remarks in *The Mass of the Roman Rite*: In ancient times the *disciplina arcani*, the discipline of the secret, was introduced to conceal the Church's holy things from the heathen outsider. But for well over a thousand years, another discipline of the secret developed whose purpose and effect was the concealment of the holy things from the faithful, from the members of the family themselves. Meditation on the passion of Christ (which was encouraged), however praiseworthy and needful, is something essentially less than active and intelligent co-offering of the Sacrifice with our High Priest, Christ.

Hand in hand with lack of participation in the offering of the Mass, due to a one-sided emphasis on the divinity of Christ, was a swift decrease in participation through reception of His Body and Blood in Holy Communion. This result occurred in both East and West. The mystery of our High Priest lovingly inviting us to share His table with Him gave place to the mystery of God deigning to make His appearance among sinful men to be adored by them. It is significant that in the very century in which worship of the Eucharist reaches a climax in the popular mind a General Council felt itself constrained to command reception of the sacrament at least once a year.

Other related areas of devotion and practice were also seriously affected by the anti-Arian stress on Christ's divinity. In general, the *sacramental view* of the Church and of Christian life was tragically obscured. If the humanity of Christ, as the first-born of many brethren, our Brother in the flesh, and as the new Head of redeemed humanity, recedes into the background in favor of His divinity, there can be no proper grasp of the *Church as the Mystical Body*, as the extension of Christ's humanity through time. And history indicates, as a matter of fact, how minor a part this doctrine played in Christian consciousness, despite the splendid theological clarities of St. Thomas on the subject.

Symptomatic of the situation is what happened at the Council of Basle (1431–39). A certain number of statements in the book of Augustine Favorini (*De sacramento unitatis Christi et Ecclesiae sive de Christo integro*), who tried to restore to honor St. Augustine's teaching on the Mystical Body, were condemned as scandalous, as "offensive to pious ears." One of the consultors of the Council, John of Torquemada, justified this procedure with the words, "Both the teachers of Christian doctrine as well as the faithful have, from their earliest youth, learned that under the name of Christ no other than the person of the Redeemer can be understood. Hence the Church cannot be described as another Christ."

If one fails to stress the *glorified humanity* of Christ, then necessarily the concept of Christ as Head of His Church becomes obscured. For then the Church will appear ever more as an earthly society, founded by Christ, yes, and helped by Him in a wonderful manner from heaven, but not as Christ incarnate in every generation. The Church then will be regarded chiefly as exercising the *authority* of Christ-God in heaven, in order to secure moral order and virtue on earth. God's authority, however, is represented on earth by the Church's hierarchy; the laity are simply and solely on the receiving end—the Church active is identified with the clerical state.

Failure to give due value to Christ's glorified humanity entailed, further, the relegation of the mystery of His resurrection to a secondary and often merely apologetic role in the totality of Christian redemption. This process has been summarized briefly by a modern author as follows:

"Once the Kyrios-dignity of the Risen One was allowed

largely to merge into and be identified with the eternal glory of
the Trinity, the Easter victory and ascension of the Saviour
came inevitably to be regarded as no more than the happy conclusion of His earthly career—and the ascension even as an
event of farewell and sorrow. Simultaneously the events of
Christ's earthly life and their relics and traces in the Holy Land
began to loom all important: for they appeared as the most
apprehensible of what the incomprehensible God in His con-
verse with man had allowed them to share. Hence the infancy
and passion accounts of Christ's life came to occupy the forefront in Christian devotion. And the redemption itself was
thought to have been realized almost exclusively in the passion.
The repercussion of these developments in regard to the earlier
Easter-centered piety of Christians is clear. Sunday, which according to the mind of the early Church was the memorial of
the resurrection, became related and has grown more explicitly
related since the Middle Ages to the incarnation and the mystery
of the Trinity (as is witnessed by the genuflection at mention
of the incarnation in the Credo, and by the assigning to Sunday, since (A.D. 800, of the votive Mass of the Trinity—of which
we still retain the Trinity preface!). The reform of Holy Week,
implemented by the theological writings of men like Durrwell
and Lyonnet, are helping us in our own day to reestablish the
balance, and once again to appreciate the climactic role of Easter
in the work of redemption, and therefore also in Christian
piety."[1]

Further, once the glad awareness of membership in the living
Body of Christ is pushed to the background, and we confront
Christ as God offended by our sins, instead of as our Elder
Brother who bore our sins *and* united us into God's own family,
man can look upon himself only *as a sinner*. Hence the multiplication of the so-called "apologies," declarations of sinfulness
that found their way from the early Middle Ages into the
liturgy, and have left some traces to our own day in the Roman
rite. God's holy people, the "saints" of St. Paul's epistles, become, so far as Christian consciousness is concerned, solely

[1] H. J. Schulz, "Die 'Höllenfahrt' als 'Anastasis'," *Zeitschrift für
katholische Theologie*, LXXI (1959), 2.

"nobis quoque peccatoribus—we sinners." It is hardly a coincidence that *grace,* ever after those times, was understood chiefly as *actual* grace, as God helping us to keep the commandments, rather than as sanctifying grace—the sharing of God's life by His adopted sons. Teachers can probably attest that such is still the predominant understanding of grace on the part of the great majority of our people. We are still, to that extent, living spiritually in terms of the Old Testament: God's servants, rather than His sons.

Parallel with the weakening of conscious belief in the saving humanity of Christ was the development in practice of the veneration of the saints. When men tend to forget the high priesthood of Christ, and remove the High Priest Himself away from contact with mankind, relegating Him to the infinite sphere of the divine, there inevitably appears a yawning gulf between man and the divine Christ, and the saints were naturally called in to bridge this gulf (cf. Karl Adam, *op. cit.,* p. 53). What effect such stressing of the divinity of Christ can have and has had in the field of Mariology has been most recently shown by Yves Congar in his booklet *Christ, Our Lady and the Church.*

For clarification it should be added that not all these developments were directly and immediately caused by an undue emphasis on the divinity of Christ. But the latter effected a theological and devotional *climate,* in which these developments, logically inherent, could then flourish and bear their fruit. And it was all too often only half-ripe fruit.

This is true especially of the subjective bent or temperament of the new Germanic peoples of the early Middle Ages, by contrast with the more objective view of realities characteristic of the world of classic times. As Karl Adam says, (in the magnificent chapter on "Christ Our Lord" in his book *Christ Our Brother*), "The sacramental objective and social elements of religion recede in favor of the moral and subjective. . . . The real basis of this veiled semi-Pelagianism lies . . . in a secret detachment from the Mystical Body of Christ, and deeper still, in the obscuration of belief in the 'first-born' of His brethren, in the Man, Christ Jesus." There results an identification of Christianity with moralism. Instead of being characterized by a joyous awareness of being a holy people of God, living in Christ and with Christ, Christianity became predominantly a moralism, a command to obey the Ten Commandments with the help of God.

Typical of this moralism was the old Saxon biblical poem, the *Heliand,* of the 9th century. It represents Christ as the liege lord, the bold Warrior, and the apostles as His faithful vassals. Discipleship of Christ is equated with loyalty: Christ is the hero and leader who through His own courage and strength inspires men to follow Him, gains their confidence, and unites them to Himself in personal bonds of fealty. When later in the Middle Ages the devout meditation on the sufferings of Christ and imitation of Him in virtuous action constituted predominantly the Christian conception of what it means to be a Christian, this conception was only the subsequent development of the *Heliand* ideal. The Church is the society, the army, of those loyal to their leader. But if loyalty is the primary bond of Christian life, then the latter is no more than a morality. There again, in effect, we are living in the climate of the Old Testament.

And this predominantly moralistic view of Christian life bore also upon the Mass, now no longer understood and participated in. The Mass became a good work to be performed by offering a stipend, or by mere attendance. The post-scholastic emphasis on the causality of the sacraments (that they effect grace *ex opere operato*—through a power in themselves) served as an additional theological encouragement for the practical elimination of the *ex opere operantis*—one's personal efforts—in holy Mass itself. The Mass to a frightening degree became an automatic device for obtaining favors, spiritual and temporal.

The great mystics, such as Master Eckhart and Tauler, roundly condemned this mechanization of Mass attendance, and constantly urged interiorization and devout assistance. The vehemence of their fight against the current externalism helps us understand some of their statements: for instance, "A single devout reflection on the passion of the Lord is worth more than a thousand Masses."

The state of affairs in the two centuries preceding Luther have been portrayed with frank objectivity in a volume by

Adolph Franz, published in 1901, *Die Messe im deutschen Mittelalter*. And a modern author, the outstanding German theologian Franz Xaver Arnold, of Tübingen, in an informative chapter in the symposium volume *Die Messe in der Glaubensverkündigung*, shows that, in an effort to correct the abuses and to help people really know what is happening at Mass, there appeared a full generation before Luther a number of prayer-books intended for the faithful, containing translations of the Ordinary and even the more important Proper parts of the Mass: something like our Sunday Missals.

These were an appeal to understanding and faith: faith based upon a better understanding. In fact, from a study of these books the German scholar, L. Pralle, concludes: "There was in the 16th century a strong, popular liturgical movement the (external) objectives of which were adopted by Luther, who thereby practically postponed the Catholic solution of the problem for centuries."

Denunciations of abuses associated with holy Mass were voiced by many individual theologians and preachers, and by a succession of diocesan synods in several lands. But most weighty of all was the voice of the committee of the Council of Trent which prepared the agenda for the Council on this subject. (The full proceedings are found in the volumes of Acts of the Council published by the Görres Gesellschaft, and they make very instructive and sobering reading.)

In its session of August 8, 1562, this committee stated: "Among the causes which, to put it mildly (*ut lenissime dicatur*), have brought about a general weakening of the power of the Mass [in Christian life], two stand out most prominently: superstition and avarice." And often, it must be admitted, avarice encouraged superstitions, especially the superstitions associated with numbered series of Masses which were thought to guarantee infallible results; dry Masses, lacking the consecration; simultaneous Masses; and especially the many theories about the fruits of the Mass. This committee, among other things, also recommended drastic reduction of votive Masses, another major evil of the time because definite and sure results were so widely attributed to them. It urged that votive Masses for the dead be forbidden on Sundays; that one and the same deacon be not permitted to serve two or three Masses simultaneously. And it recommended that fewer Masses be celebrated "lest too large a number of priests and sacraments arouse contempt." Too large a number of priests! As Lortz in his standard work on the Protestant Reformation, *Die Reformation in Deutschland*, states: "There was a clerical proletariat of fearful strength in respect to numbers, but also of fearfully low quality." In Breslau, toward the end of the 15th century, no less than 236 priests were attached to two of the town's churches, solely as "altar priests," whose only duty it was to celebrate foundation Masses. And he estimates that nearly one-twentieth of the inhabitants of the towns belonged to the ranks of the clergy.

The Council of Trent undertook the essential measures to right the state of affairs. The uniform missal, resulting from Trent, even dropped the rite of the offertory procession—which in itself might have been very instructive to underscore the principle of the laity's participation. It was dropped because it was felt that it, likewise, offered too much occasion for continued superstition about guaranteeing results from the Mass and trafficking with sacred things.

But by the time the Council acted, the damage had been done. The mechanization of Masses, all too often for the sake of clerical financial gain, had been an easy target of attack in the name of honest religion.

In his decisive work *On the Babylonian Captivity* (1520), Luther could point to the *opus operatum* idea (explained by him as the Mass mechanically producing its results without reference to the personal piety or devotion of those attending) as one of the *monstra impietatis,* the "monstrous impieties" that characterized the Church.

His appeal to the necessity of faith, of personal surrender to Christ, was so reasonable (and, in the circumstances, so *new*), that one can understand why his preaching had such a powerful appeal, why it swept all before it, seemingly like a great new tide of spiritual renewal, of personal dedication to Christ. What he called for was in fact a sound Catholic principle—though tragically divorced from the *total* picture. And his appeal was all the more successful because he touched the people where it was most painful—in their pocketbooks—by denouncing the Mass as "spiritual traffic based on clerical cupidity."

And, so, in one generation it was accomplished. In *one* generation a large percentage of the German people had been persuaded that the Mass, which up to that time they had accepted as the most precious possession of their Christian faith, is impious idolatry, destructive of all true piety. Had the Mass been understood, had the faithful been taught to offer themselves with Christ and so, in consequence, to transform their daily lives, the Protestant Reformation could not have happened—at least not in the manner and to the extent that it did. They rejected what they knew not.

Small wonder that a prominent German Lutheran theologian of our day, Hans Asmussen, has declared that the traditional Protestant arguments against the Mass can no longer be applied *tale quale* to Pope Pius XII's explanation of the Sacrifice in *Mediator Dei.*

And the lesson to be drawn from all this? "What think ye of Christ?" In this century the vicars of Christ—the three Piuses, and Pope John—have answered this question in a manner and with an insistence that speaks not only to theologians but to God's entire holy people, and have thereby initiated what Pope Pius XII declared to be a "springtime" in the life of the Church.

SELECT BIBLIOGRAPHY

The following bibliography is germane to the specific points raised in this section of the book and we would like to draw the reader's attention to it.

Karl Adam, *Christ Our Brother* (New York: 1931), chap. "Through Christ Our Lord."

F. X. Arnold, *Grundsätzliches und geschichtliches zur Theologie der Seelsorge* (Freiburg: 1949).

———, "Bleibt der Laie ein Stiefkind der Kirche?" *Hochland,* XLVI (1954), 401–12; 524–33.

F. X. Arnold and Balthasar Fischer, *Die Messe in der Glaubensverkündigung* (Freiburg: 1950).

Edmund Bishop, *Liturgica Historica* (Oxford: 1918), chaps. VIII and VIIIa.

Louis Bouyer, *Liturgical Piety* (Notre Dame: 1954), chaps. 1–5.

P. Browe, *Die Verehrung der Eucharistie im Mittelalter* (Münster: 1933).

Yves Congar, *Lay People in the Church* (Westminster: 1957).

E. Dumoutet, *Le Christ selon la Chair et la Vie Liturgique au Moyen-Age* (Paris: 1932).

F. X. Durrwell, *La Résurrection du Christ, Mystère de Salut* (2nd ed., Paris: 1955).

Stephanus Ehses (ed.), *Concilii Tridentini Actorum*, Pars Quinta: Vol. VIII (Freiburg: 1919).

A. Franz, *Die Messe im Deutschen Mittelalter* (Freiburg: 1902).

Ildefons Herwegen, *Antike, Germanentum und Christentum* (Salzburg: 1932).

———, *Kirche und Seele* (Münster: 1926).

Hubert Jedin, "Das Konzil von Trient und die Reform des Römischen Messbuches," *Liturgisches Leben*, VI (1939), 30–66.

J. A. Jungmann, *Die Frohbotschaft und unsere Glaubensverkündigung* (Regensburg: 1936).

———, *The Mass of the Roman Rite*, Vol. I (New York: 1950), pp. 7–167.

———, "Die Abwehr des Germanischen Arianismus und der Umbruch der religiösen Kultur im frühen Mittelalter," *Zeitschrift für katholische Theologie*, LXIX (1947), 36–99.

———, "The Pastoral Idea in the History of the Liturgy," *Assisi Papers* (Collegeville: 1957), pp. 18–31.

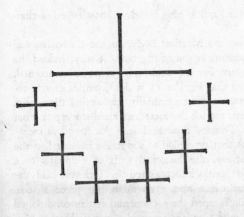

PART TWO

I. TWO APPROACHES TO UNDERSTANDING
THE SACRAMENTS

A revered confrere, Patrick Cummins, O.S.B., of Conception
Abbey, likes to tell that his interest in the liturgical movement
was aroused many years ago by his study of St. Thomas, especially his questions on the sacraments in the *Summa
Theologica*.

This may come as a surprise to many of us. We are quite
willing to make a reverential bow towards St. Thomas in every
problem of theology. But we also know that there have been
some notable developments of theological thought since his
time. In our own day, besides the important field of Mariology,
the doctrine of the Mystical Body and, as a consequence, the
thinking about the sacraments, i.e., the liturgy, have been in
the forefront of theological concern. Especially since Pius XII's
encyclical on the Mystical Body and his *Mediator Dei*, they
have led to vitally significant new insights into God's plan of
redemption. Their impact on Christian life is, in fact, a primary

feature of the spiritual quickening widely acknowledged as characterizing our age.

This emphasis on the Mystical Body, on the Eucharist, and on the other sacraments is something new. It may, indeed, be called a new discovery. For it is such so far as we are concerned. But I am convinced that Fr. Patrick is right, particularly in respect to the sacraments. Our spiritually stimulating discoveries about the sacraments are for the most part a rediscovery of what is contained in St. Thomas' *Summa Theologica* for all to see.

The trouble was that we failed to see it. As indicated in the preceding Introduction, the historical shift of emphasis to a more individualistic outlook occasioned by Ockham and the philosophy of Nominalism and, even more, our preoccupation with Protestant attacks upon the sacramental system conditioned our thinking. We might say they proved a mental block which led us to look for, and to find, only those things which served our purposes—largely apologetic. In a word, we did not approach the *Summa* with an open mind.

It is really exhilarating, after reading modern liturgical-theological writings on the sacraments, to turn to questions 60–65 of the Third Part of the *Summa Theologica* (in which St. Thomas treats of the sacraments in general) and to realize that it is basically all there: not of course developed and explicit in every detail, but easily recognizable in his principles, and presented with that balance of component elements which is his chief merit in treating the sacraments.

It is quite as it should be, therefore, that most of the outstanding modern theological authors whose writings on the sacraments have stimulated and are stimulating the liturgical apostolate base their thinking squarely and frankly on St. Thomas: Vonier, Héris, Roguet, Journet, Congar, Philipon, and above all Schillebeeckx in his important new volumes, and Vagaggini in his *The Theological Dimensions of the Liturgy*. These men have rediscovered St. Thomas' key position in the development of sacramental theology, because they have recognized how St. Thomas insisted on, and maintained, the proper relation and balance between sign and causality in treating of the sacraments.

Sign and causality: these are the operative words in sacramental theology. The entire history of theology concerning the sacraments revolves around them. A sacrament is defined in our catechisms as "an external sign instituted by Christ, which confers grace." There we have the two terms: "sign" and "confers" (i.e. causes) the grace which it signifies.

In the chapter "Christ in the Liturgy" I shall again deal with the sacraments. But preliminarily, in this chapter, it is my purpose to sketch briefly how before St. Thomas the emphasis was on sign, and how after him it has been too one-sidedly on causality, and then to show how this imbalance since St. Thomas' day has led to an impoverished view of the sacraments and their role in the spiritual life—a view which is being rectified only in our own day and which has necessitated a liturgical movement or, as it is perhaps better named, a sacramental apostolate.

The history of sacramental thinking can be found in such a standard work as Pourrat's *Theology of the Sacraments,* or in Albert Michel's extensive study of "Sacraments" and "Sacramentals" in *Dictionnaire de Théologie Catholique.* We cannot hope here to do more than sketch the briefest outline, at the obvious peril of over-simplification.

Quoting Pourrat, we can say that "in the first four centuries, the Church administered the sacraments without theorizing about them" (p. 396). For the next eight centuries, following St. Augustine, who was the first to attempt a technical definition of a sacrament—"a sacrament is a sign of grace"—theological thought was dominated by the sign or signification aspect of the sacrament. The scholastics of the twelfth century, whose thinking was climaxed and balanced by St. Thomas, "completed the Augustinian formula by adding the specific idea: a sacrament is an *efficacious* sign of grace"—i.e., the sacraments *cause* what they signify. And St. Thomas' personal great contribution lies in his exposition of how the sacraments are instrumental causes.

After Thomas, or roughly during the last seven centuries, theological interest has centered on the causality of the sacraments. To quote Vagaggini: theology after Thomas, "and especially since the sixteenth century, in the treatment of the sacraments in general and in particular, has so relegated the concept of sign to second place that it has, practically speaking, forgotten it or, at least, has left it inoperative" (p. 464).

In brief—and necessarily omitting nuances—we can therefore speak of four introductory centuries, eight centuries of priority of sign, a brief period centering around Thomas which clarifies the concept of causality and relates it and balances it with that of sign, and then seven centuries of an unbalanced emphasis on causality.

What relevance has this for our spiritual life? To clear the ground, it may be necessary first of all to belabor the obvious.

A sacrament is a sign. St. Thomas did not think it a waste of time to devote his entire first question (60) with its eight articles to this statement; it runs, moreover, like a decisive motif through all his treatment of the sacraments.

A sign, he tells us, quoting St. Augustine's definition, is an object, the external perception of which suggests the idea of something else. The aim, the sole aim, of a sign is to suggest an idea, to call something to mind. In a word, to instruct. In the case of the sacraments it is Christ who instructs, insofar as He chose the sign; and it is the Church too that instructs, inasmuch as she expanded and further explained the essential sign, by surrounding it with additional rites and prayers. No one less than Christ and the Church themselves, therefore, are our teachers about sacraments and about their purpose and role in the divine dispensation. We could wish for no more competent teachers, and we can be confident that they teach us what is important for us to know as Christians.

Josef Jungmann, S.J., in fact, has shown that during the early centuries of the Church the liturgy was the *only* means by which Christians were normally instructed. The sacramental sign of the Eucharist, of the sacraments and the other liturgical celebrations constituted the only school in which the Church taught her children the truths of faith.

To understand this rather startling statement we must recall, however, that the phrase sacramental "sign" is here interpreted in its traditional sense, embracing not only the essential matter and form, but all the supplementary rites, prayers, readings, and homilies that pertained to it. Thus, in the case of baptism and the other sacraments of initiation, it would include the richly instructive content of what we call the Lenten season, the entire catechumenate together with its sermon-instructions, the blessing of the water, and even the Masses and homilies after Easter. All these belonged to the sign of baptism through which the Church instructed the candidates.

It is particularly important to recall this fact that the sign consisted not merely of the sacramental rites and prayers. The sermons or homilies were a normal part of the liturgy. And it is significant that it is precisely during these centuries, even though the prayers were in a language understood by the people, and the rites undoubtedly more easily intelligible to them than they are to us, that SS. Cyril of Jerusalem, Ambrose, Augustine, and many others explained the rites and prayers of the sacraments of initiation in magnificent series of sermons that have come down to our day. As ministers of the mysteries of God, they knew it was their duty not only to explain the word of God contained in Scripture, but also the word, the teaching of Christ and the Church, contained in the sacramental sign. They had to help their people to read the sign.

For the same reason, the Council of Trent decreed: "That the faithful may approach the sacraments with greater reverence and devotion of mind, the holy council commands all bishops not only that when they are themselves about to administer them to the people, they shall first, in a manner adapted to the mental ability of those who receive them, explain their efficacy and use, but also that they shall see to it that the same is done piously and prudently by every parish priest, and in the vernacular tongue . . ." (Sess. 24, chap. 7).

The Ritual, as we know, reiterates this command of the Council (Tit. I, 10). "In the administration of the sacraments," it says, their power, use and purpose and the meaning of the rites must be diligently explained.

A second principle to recall, and one much stressed by St. Thomas, is that sacraments *significando causant*—by signifying they cause. Or, as it was formulated later, sacraments cause what they signify. The sign, therefore, comes first and must remain so. For the causality is co-extensive with, and determined by the sign. The sign is not just an interesting phenomenon which happens to be attached to sacraments (Hugh of St. Victor). Rather, only a correct and full reading of the sign can tell us what is being caused.

Important? An example: because the sign of the Eucharist, namely, food, daily strengthening spiritual food, was relegated to secondary prominence by other considerations, stemming originally from reaction to the Arian heresy in the fourth century, as explained in the Introduction, fifteen centuries of Christians were deprived of frequent Communion. There was no question of denial of truth; but the basic lesson of the sign was not generally heeded. Consequently, values were out of focus.

Perhaps we can now proceed to an analysis, however sketchy, of some of the historical consequences in spiritual life and outlook that resulted from neglecting St. Thomas' balance of sign and causality, and from a too exclusive concern with the latter during approximately the past seven centuries.

A first result can be seen in a certain obscuring in the minds of Catholics of the role and importance of faith in the process of salvation. (In the following I must oversimplify in the interests of brevity; so I hope that the theologians among my readers will make the necessary allowances in what I say.) No need to enumerate the many Scripture texts which speak of the faith that saves. But also, only "he who believes and is baptized shall be saved." What is the relation, then, between faith and baptism, or faith and the sacraments? Are we saved by faith, or are we saved by baptism and the other sacraments?

For St. Thomas there was no problem. Faith and sacraments are not two separate compartments, as it were, vying with each other for priority. Repeatedly and as a matter of course he speaks of the sacraments as "signs of faith," "signs proclaiming or expressing faith." The sacraments themselves are the great acts of faith. (Both Vonier in his *Key to the Doctrine of the Eucharist* and Roguet in his *Christ Acts through the Sacraments* treat this subject well.) Sacraments, as signs, are acts of faith of the Church, first of all. But they are also the great acts of faith of the individual Christian. Moreover, active and understanding participation in the sacraments, besides manifesting the faith of the individual Christian, also deepens and develops it. There is no opposition, or a question of either-or. The faith which is the root of all justification must be manifested in the manner prescribed by Christ Himself, i.e., by the sacraments. The sacraments (especially baptism and the

Eucharist) are the acts of faith demanded by Christ. Thus St. Thomas in treating of baptism, for instance, no less than fifteen times simply calls it *sacramentum fidei*, the sacrament or sign of faith.

Subsequent neglect of the sign, with relative overemphasis on the causality of the sacraments as producing grace, was bound to result in an overshadowing of the role of faith in the popular mind, and in a corresponding naïve isolation of the sacraments as channels of grace. With what explosive results—we witness in the Protestant Reformation. In fact, Lortz in his volumes on the *Reformation in Germany* echoes other authors in wondering whether the Protestant Reformation could have had such spectacular success if Trent's clarifying statement on faith and justification had been promulgated—and preached and understood—before the revolt.

A second result of an unthomistically one-sided stress on causality was a more or less mechanistic view of the sacraments. This, perhaps the most baneful, result is still doing its damage today. I believe the average view of the sacraments is something like the following: The sacraments produce grace *ex opere operato*, by their very conferring. Christ instituted them, yes; but entrusted them to the Church. And the Church guarantees the results, relying on the word of Christ. The sacrament is a holy *thing* which contains and confers grace. If matter and form are there, the result is infallible. We shall have more to say on this matter in the following chapter. Meanwhile, we must make this point:

Despite all our protestations to the contrary, it sounds like magic. And there can be no doubt that, in practice, sacraments were regarded in this mechanistic fashion by vast sections of the faithful before the Reformation. Superstitious uses of sacraments abounded. To all intents and purposes, they *were* medicine chests. The Protestant accusation that sacraments are a manmade machinery interposed between Christ and the soul, the Protestant revolt against sacramentalism, and Protestants' appeal for a personal religion, a religion of personal union with Christ, could not have found a willing audience otherwise. Luther's denunciations of the *ex opere operato* were justified if we recognize how that term was then widely understood, and how not a few of our people, it is to be feared, understand it today.

Reflection on the sign, on the essential forms—This is *My Body*, *I baptize you*, *I absolve you*—the pronouns can refer only to Christ—makes such a mechanistic view impossible. Christ is not merely the distant historical Christ who founded the sacraments two thousand years ago. To say He instituted the sacraments means that He chose these signs through which He has willed Himself, here in the present, to effect salvation. The sacraments are not things: they are actions, the saving actions of Christ. This is what St. Thomas clarifies by the philosophical concept of sacraments being instrumental causes. *Ex opere operato* means really, *ex opere operantis Christi*—sacraments effect grace because they are the actions of Christ.

We must be grateful that Pius XII in *Mediator Dei* again put primary emphasis on this fact. The sacraments, he says repeatedly, are the continuation in the present of the priestly activity of Christ. Or again: "Christ is present in the sacraments, infusing into them the power which makes them ready instruments of sanctification" (20). Pius XII again *personalized* the sacraments in a way that makes impossible any mechanistic misconception. If that emphasis had been present in the sixteenth century, one wonders whether the Protestant revolt would ever have amounted to more than a local theological dispute in a provincial university.

A third historical result of over-stressing causality to the detriment of sign was that the sign was narrowed down even more by theologians to what was essential *ad validitatem*, for validity. "What is necessary for validity" became the decisive question in theology textbooks, rather than: "What does the *full* sign teach about the effects of this sacrament?" In other words, what is the legitimate concern of the moral theologian and the canonist has been substituted for the broader considerations of dogmatic theology in our textbooks. Vagaggini in his recent study has documented this fact in the case of every well-known dogmatic theology manual since Trent. Not one of them bases its treatment on an inquiry into the full sign—a sign given to us for our instruction by Christ and the Church in the wealth of sacramental rites and prayers. And theologians write our catechisms.

Again it was Pius XII who called a halt to viewing the sacramental sign solely in terms of what is essential *ad validitatem*. In his constitution on holy orders (1947) he points out the essential words in the ordination rites of deacons, priests, and bishops, but he calls the entire respective preface the "form" of the sacrament.

The fourth spiritual disadvantage resulting from the utilitarian emphasis on causality at the expense of sign is illustrated by the interpretation commonly given to a phrase used by the Council of Trent: *non ponentibus obicem*. "If anyone says that the sacraments of the New Law do not contain the grace which they signify, or that they do not confer that grace on those who place no obstacles in the way . . . let him be anathema" (Sess. VII, Can. 6. Denz. 849).

What the Council obviously intended with this canon was to safeguard the basic truth that the grace of the sacraments is caused, not in any way by man, but by the sacraments themselves, that is to say, by Christ acting through the sacraments. Man cannot merit saving grace, which is a gift of God's sheer mercy. The phrase itself, "not placing a hindrance," the Council took over from St. Augustine (Ep. 98:10), who used it in regard to infants, who, he points out, cannot personally place a hindrance to the effects of the sacrament of baptism and therefore receive it fruitfully. The Council applies parallel thinking to all the sacraments: it is not the personal merit of the recipient that causes the grace received. On the other hand, God does not force the human will.

And so the Council's declaration has passed over into our common definition of a sacrament, "An external sign, instituted by Christ, which confers grace on those who do not place an obstacle."

What does such a definition convey to the average Catholic? My own experience in teaching on several levels is that ten out of ten will understand it to mean: "All that I have to do in order to receive the graces of the sacraments is *not* to place an obstacle: i.e., not to be in mortal sin." The impression given by the definition is that of passivity on the part of the recipient.

Certainly such an impression was furthest from the Council's mind. The Council was defining essential truths, defining also what was necessary for the validity of the sacrament. It was not

intending to give a full description of how the sacraments are
to be received. It did this eloquently, and at length, elsewhere,
especially in speaking of baptism and penance. Man cannot
contribute to causing the grace of the sacraments; but, to cite
an example, the closer a man approaches to fire, the more he
will be warmed; so also, the better a man is disposed for the
reception of a sacrament (which disposition itself of course is
possible only through grace), the more fruitfully he will receive the sacrament.

The Council was stating a minimum. By our one-sided stress
on causality, we have made its declaration into a norm about
receiving the sacraments. "Valid" and "worthy" reception have
become synonymous. The Council itself, following St. Thomas,
elsewhere insisted on the sign, on the faith which the Church
wishes to arouse and quicken in the recipient by the sign, by the
prayers and rites of the sacrament. St. Thomas, for his part, does
not use the phrase "not placing an obstacle." He knows the
doctrine, of course. But in speaking of the recipient, he consistently refers to the sign of the sacrament, and how it is meant
to dispose one more perfectly for receiving the sacramental
graces. He calls for an interior conversion to God, for a personal
encounter between the soul and its Savior. Receiving the sacrament must be a personal act of faith and submission to God's
redeeming love.

Rarely does St. Thomas speak of "valid reception": he is
more concerned with emphasizing the positive *recta dispositio*—
the right disposition, worthy of a Christian. We often seem to
be more interested in teaching the minimum than in urging
the optimum. This is not how saints are made, and sacraments
are supposed to make saints.

Fides et devotio: faith and devotion (self-surrender), St.
Thomas calls for—incidentally, the very words used in the
Canon of the Mass concerning God's holy people. Not only in
regard to the Eucharist; of the recipients of every sacrament,
St. Thomas expects that their faith be known to God, and their
self-surrender manifest. And, to repeat, it is chiefly by the sign
of the sacrament that he presupposes such faith and devotion
to be stirred up. To cite but one instance: since the sacrament
is a sign of Christ's passion, we too must be ready and willing

to enter into, to be conformed to, Christ's passion in our innermost wills and daily life.

This is clearly an entirely different spiritual climate from the largely passive, if not outright mechanistic, view of the sacraments that concentrates on their causing grace in those not placing an obstacle. The Church *must* be concerned with encouraging the right disposition of faith and self-surrender; for she cannot forget that Christ too on earth was eager to work His most generous signs and wonders in favor of those whose faith was great.

Another area in which the neglect of the sign aspect of the sacraments has had repercussions is the area of the sacramentals. In the following chapter we shall have more to say about sacramentals; our present object is to speak of them insofar as they are *signs*. It is generally known that until the twelfth century all outward signs of grace were called simply sacraments. Distinction of course was made between the major sacraments, the more important signs according to Holy Scripture and traditional theology, and the minor sacraments, the signs which are of obviously less significance in the life of the Church. It was Peter Lombard who laid down the principles which, for all posterity, clearly distinguished between the seven major signs, called sacraments, and the multiple minor signs which henceforth were known as sacramentals.

Now, if we approach the question of sacraments and sacramentals primarily from the standpoint of their causality, their distinction looms large, and rightly so. For only the sacraments confer grace *ex opere operato*—by their very conferring. And because the stress since St. Thomas has been one-sidedly on causality, the valid and necessary distinction between sacraments and sacramentals has resulted in what amounts to an undue separation of these two kinds of sacred signs. Sacraments confer grace, and therefore they are all-important, in a category all by themselves. Whereas sacramentals, which do not of themselves confer grace—what of them? In contrast to sacraments, they seem not to amount to much.

Theologically they have become therefore seriously neglected —just try to find an adequate treatment of sacramentals in any theology textbook. And yet sacramentals constitute the greater bulk of one of the basic liturgical books of the Church, the Ritual. This theological neglect has led to a corresponding neglect in practice. And so far as explaining them is concerned, our principal aim would almost seem to be to avoid any danger of superstition by insisting that their effectiveness is *ex opere operantis*, i.e., depending on the disposition of the user.

In a word, we have quite thoroughly isolated the sacramentals. They are a world apart, a world we do not exactly know what to do with. There is even a modern trend in theology of denying the name sacramental to the rites and prayers surrounding the essential matter and form of each sacrament.

We forget that there is another way of viewing sacramentals, the way of St. Thomas, the way of the sign. St. Thomas has no special treatment on the sacramentals, but he brings them in constantly in connection with his treatment of the sacraments. He views the entire sacramental system, including the sacramentals, as a unified whole, with the Eucharist as the source and center, the other sacraments surrounding it, and the sacramentals, all of them, relating to the sacraments, and ultimately to the Eucharist, as disposing man for the sacraments. Thus the catechumenate, or the exorcisms before baptism, are signs of faith, or of rejection of Satan and sin, effectively preparing man to receive the grace of baptism itself. All sacramentals, moreover, not merely the rites and prayers of Mass or the other sacraments, are expressions, signs, of our faith in the saving action of Christ, and therefore to some degree share in bringing it to man. They assist the sacraments in doing their uniquely essential work. They belong, as minor ministers, to the hierarchy of the sacramental world.

I am not, God forbid, trying to erase the essential difference between sacraments and sacramentals. But I am saying that if we regard sacramentals as sacred signs, chosen for the most part by the Church in order to stir faith and devotion in the faithful with a view to their reception of the sacraments, we will rescue the sacramentals from their isolation, and fit them again into the total pattern of Christ *and* the Church acting to save us through signs.

Greater emphasis on sacramentals as signs, signs of the faith of the Church, and not only of the faith of the Christian who uses them, will consequently result even in crediting them with greater effectiveness than we have hitherto been inclined to attribute to them. No longer will we be tempted to regard them as working solely *ex opere operantis* of the faithful—i.e., the personal effort of the recipient or user. Pius XII in *Mediator Dei* says: "their effectiveness is due rather to the action of the Church (*ex opere operantis Ecclesiae*), inasmuch as she is holy and acts always in closest union with her Head" (27). It is of considerable significance for the theology of sacramentals that this phrase, *ex opere operantis Ecclesiae* (by the action of the Church), a phrase much used and urged by liturgists, was here used, it would seem, for the first time in an official document of the teaching Church (cf. Vagaggini, p. 97).

In fact, this encyclical should be a major impetus to a theological rediscovery of the importance of the sacramentals. As a consequence of viewing sacraments and sacramentals too exclusively from the pragmatic standpoint of efficacy, we have associated sacraments with Christ (external signs, instituted by Christ, etc.) and sacramentals with the Church (external signs, instituted by the Church, etc.)—thus, as it were, divorcing Christ from His bride, at least in the minds of our faithful. Pius XII however states: "Along with the Church, her divine Founder is present at every liturgical function" (20). And then he explicitly applies the principle to the sacramentals of the divine office and the liturgical year: "Christ is present in the prayer of praise and petition we direct to God" (20). And: "The liturgical year . . . is not a cold and lifeless representation of the events of the past. . . . It is rather Christ Himself who is ever living in His Church. Here He continues that journey of immense mercy which He lovingly began in His mortal life, going about doing good" (165).

That is to say, not only sacraments, but sacramentals too, are in their own minor but supplementary way a continuation of the priestly activity of Christ Himself. To use the simile of the late Dr. Pinsk: sacramentals cannot be less than the hem of Christ's garment, from which too, as the Evangelist records, power went forth.

Other areas in which a return to St. Thomas' balance between the sign and causality of sacraments would enrich our spiritual vision can only be briefly alluded to. Yet each of them is of such importance that it would deserve full treatment.

There is, first of all, the social character and role of the sacraments. Viewing the sacraments primarily in terms of causality has inevitably led to the rather individualistic outlook of: "What does this sacrament give me individually? What graces do I get out of baptism, penance, Holy Communion?" Yet the whole of tradition, embodied and proclaimed in the sign, i.e., the prayers and rites of the sacraments, urges that every sacrament involves the whole Church: that every sacrament, and especially the Eucharist, is a bond that unites the whole Church and member to member; that the Mystical Body is a *communio sanctorum*, an organism of sacraments; that she is constituted by sacraments, lives and grows and flourishes through the sacraments; that baptism is not only membership in Christ, but is such because first of all it is membership in Christ's Body; that the purpose of the Eucharist is, to use St. Thomas' favorite phrase, "the unity of the Mystical Body."

This social character of the sacraments is moreover eloquently borne out by the sign of the sacraments insofar as it tells of the relation established through the sacraments between the individual Christians and their common father in God, the bishop of the diocese. This relationship with the bishop through sacraments was highlighted again by Pius XII through his reform of Holy Week, especially by the prominence restored to the Mass of Holy Chrism on Maundy Thursday.

Sacraments are signs of salvation, yes; but salvation is in and through the Church.

A modern English theologian, Bernard Leeming, S.J. (*Principles of Sacramental Theology*) has therefore even ventured to attempt what he considers a better definition of sacraments: "Might not a sacrament be better defined as 'an effective sign of a particular form of union with the Mystical Body, the Church, instituted by Jesus Christ, which gives grace to those who receive it rightly'?"

At all events it is not just a coincidence that underestimation of the social character of the sacraments as embodied in their sign runs parallel, historically, with the gradual loss of awareness or obscuring of the doctrine of the Mystical Body. Conversely, what might be called the rediscovery of the Mystical Body in our own time has meant a corresponding discovery of the role of the sacraments in Christian life. The encyclical on the Mystical Body was continued logically, as Pius XII himself said, by the encyclical on the liturgy.

Another new (or restored) insight of our day, consequent upon studying the sign of the sacraments, has been a better realization that all the sacraments—and sacramentals—are not merely means of sanctification (i.e., important because of their effect on man), but are basically and intrinsically worship. Emphasis on causality, on effect, has given rise to the axiom *Sacramenta propter homines*. Sacraments are for man. True. But this is only half the truth. As Cardinal Suhard reminded us in his *The Meaning of God*:

"The expansive phrase is often repeated, and rightly, sacraments are for men. But it is not sufficiently realized that if the reception of the sacraments must always be made possible to the faithful, the reason is that they can thus the better appropriate them and be carried along in the great movement of praise and thanksgiving rising from this earth to God through His Son. If the sacraments are emptied of this essential content they will soon become lifeless rites."

Sacraments are for man: but man is for God. Or, as Pius XII said succinctly in *Mediator Dei*: "Let everything, therefore, have its proper place and arrangement; let everything be 'theocentric' so to speak" (33). To how many of our faithful would it nowadays occur that receiving the sacrament of penance is worship? Yet the sign of the sacrament is intended to arouse "faith and devotion" (self-surrender), the root and primary act respectively of the virtue of religion, which is worship. The indelible characters or signs of baptism, confirmation, and holy orders are deputations to worship. St. Thomas therefore, in summarizing the purpose of the sacraments says quite indiscrimately: "They are for the sanctification of man" or "they perfect man in those things which pertain to the worship of God"—as if these two ideas were interchangeable. And they are. For by active and intelligent participation in the sacraments, man is lifted out of his own narrow self-centeredness, to become one with Christ. And Christ gave His life for the salvation of man—but in order that, together with His new brethren, He may now give glory to the Father.

This view of sacraments certainly widens our horizons, frees us from a suffocating spiritual selfishness. Peace, grace, to men of good will, yes—but for the purpose of giving glory to God.

Two final ways in which St. Thomas' balance between sign and cause would profit our spiritual maturity I can no more than mention. The Church in her sacramental signs steeps us in biblical thought. She loves to recall the signs and sacraments of the Old Testament, and the signs and wonders of Christ in the New. Liturgy and Scripture are blood brothers. And a true understanding of the liturgy would again make us Bible Christians—a consummation devoutly to be wished.

Finally, reflection on the sacramental sign would bring back more vividly to our consciousness the eschatological nature of our Christian existence; i.e., it would bring heaven and our eternal goal into the present. Concentration on the graces received here and now has made us forget more or less that, as St. Thomas insists, every sacrament as a sign signifies, not only present graces, but the past, the passion and death of Christ, and the future, eternal glory. It is well to remind our faithful: "Remember thy last end, and thou shalt not sin." But it is by means of the sacraments that the Church herself gives that reminder to the active and understanding participant. Every sacrament should make us less earthbound, should, may I say, give us wings. Every sacrament, since it actually confers the seed of eternal glory, should make us homesick for our eternal home, should lift up our hearts, for we are in fact, and not only in hope, citizens of heaven. Every sacrament is a joyful *sursum corda*.

Keeping in mind the further development of these concepts, given in the next chapter, I have tried to outline principles, and have not discussed practice, except incidentally. What practical conclusion would I draw from this discussion? That the sacramental apostolate, if properly understood and realized in practice, does have major contributions to make to a fuller and more mature Christian life and outlook. Sacraments are formative of the will, and also of the mind. They are not sufficient by themselves, however, in their teaching. It would be foolish—and very likely fatal—to depend solely on the sacramental sign, no matter how broadly interpreted. No responsible liturgist, so far as I know, is advocating this.

But Pius XI did say: "The liturgy is the most important organ of the ordinary magisterium (i.e., teaching power) of the Church." Not the only, but the most important. Far from being exclusivists, we liturgists want to be inclusivists: we want (we honestly believe) what the Church wants: that the liturgy, after seven centuries of relative neglect as a teaching organ, be again more fully included in the normal teaching activity of parish school and church, and that its instructional and spiritually formative wealth, put there by Christ Himself and the Church, be exploited to a greater degree than it has been.

II. CHRIST IN THE LITURGY

Any priest, any "minister of the mysteries of God," who is called upon to speak of these same mysteries, will humbly echo in his soul the beautiful words of the Apostle: "Yes, to me, the very least of all the saints, there was given this grace, to announce among (you) the good tidings of the unfathomable riches of Christ, . . . the dispensation of the mystery which has been hidden from eternity in God . . . in order that through the Church there be made known . . . the eternal purpose which he accomplished in Christ Jesus our Lord" (Eph. 3:8–11).

In the preceding chapter, we considered the sacraments and the sacramentals insofar as they are signs, and not just spiritual medicines of some kind intended to produce their optimum effect merely by the taking. Thus we have prepared the way to showing in this chapter that, far from being just prescriptions left by the Divine Physician with the Church as a spiritual pharmacy (though there is something in that analogy if properly understood), they continue to be the manifold personal ministration of the Good Samaritan who is our Saviour.

Liturgical Week 1950, Conception, Mo.

That the liturgy, or the sacramental world, must be taught to consist first and above all in nothing less than the prolongation of the priestly mission of Jesus Christ was stressed by Pius XII in the first part of his encyclical "On the Liturgy" (NCWC edition, nos. 3, 17, 18, 20, 22). The liturgy—sacrifice, sacraments and sacramentals—"is nothing more nor less than the exercise of (Christ's) priestly function" (no. 22). The liturgical movement, therefore, is nothing more nor less than an effort to translate the theology of the sacraments into practice in a way most conformable to the glory of God and the salvation of souls.

If—as it exists in all the well-known manuals—"the theology of the sacraments" has largely consisted (by Vagaggini's findings already cited) in the canonico-moral aspects of a kind of spiritual pharmacopoeia, may I suggest that, with all the current talk about the revision of these manuals and about the need of making theology come to life, the section on the sacraments stands most in need of "rejuvenation," of reflecting the considerable scholarly work of modern theologians and liturgists to gain a deeper insight into the meaning and role of the sacraments, and, above all, of following the authoritative example of emphases given by *Mediator Dei*. It seems an intolerable anomaly that what some have regarded as the "driest and deadest tract in theology" should be the very one which treats of the communication of divine life.

Now before going on to a further discussion of the relation of sacraments to Christ and the relation of sacramentals to sacraments, I wish to express my conviction that in both instances there has been too much separation in our thinking concerning them. Such separation represents, according to many thinkers, a typical Western, and more particularly post-scholastic, weakness. We distinguish, we separate things in our minds, for the sake of logical systematization—and then fail to put them properly together again. The result is that "fragmentation" of which Maritain wrote in *Commonweal* some years ago as a chief disease of our civilization. We see things piecemeal; we lose the vision of the whole. Hence the feverish search for "integration," as for instance in the field of education. When this departmentalizing takes over in the field of theology or the spiritual life, it can be especially harmful. I need but remind readers of the

American hierarchy's statement several years ago on secularism. I must insist that if the vision of the whole is obscured, Christian life becomes all too easily (and tragically) a *sum total* of, say, 170 truths and 2414 laws. We lose sight of the fact that Christianity is not so much a hundred or more facts, but one sole fact, one sole all-embracing reality: Christianity is Christ, the Son of God made man, living in and through His Body, the Church. And once we get lost in detail, at the expense of the central vision, Christian life almost inevitably becomes a series of laborious duties, a treadmill—instead of its being the Gospel, the joy-creating tidings that the apostles preached. In other words, this is not just a theological problem, but very decidedly a spiritual problem. But now let us return to the topic of this chapter.

The June 1948, issue of the English Dominican *Life of the Spirit* quotes "a famous professor at the Angelicum" to the effect that we have in recent centuries tended to divorce the sacraments too much from Christ. This same concern is being voiced by more and more students of the sacraments: e.g., Graber, *Christus in seinen heiligen Sakramenten;* F. X. Arnold, *Theologie der Seelsorge.*

We have already indicated one reason for this divorce: our view of sacraments as guaranteed capsules of grace (grace being thought of in turn simply as a "help" to getting to heaven). But it will also cast light on this divorce to reconsider the parallel estrangement in our view of Christ and Church: In a 1948 "Bulletin on Ecclesiology" in the *Revue des sciences philosophiques et théologiques* the French Dominican Yves Congar briefly sketched the historical reasons why this happened in the theology on the Church: "The modern tractate on the Church was formed by reaction and defense against a series of errors (Wycliffe's, Hus's, the Reformers', Gallicanism, Jansenism, laicism, state absolutism), errors which strained everything in one direction. The doctrine on the Church became principally, at times almost exclusively, a defense and declaration of the Church's reality (and rights) as a *society,* as a perfect society, a defense of her hierarchical constitution, of the powers and primacy of the Holy See." Experience shows how true this judgment of Father Congar is—so much so that we can even speak of a "rediscovery" of the Church as the Mystical Body! It may sound amusing now, but it is indicative of a state of affairs, that at the Council of the Vatican some of those present wanted in fact to have the doctrine of the Mystical Body condemned as savoring of modernism!

Some of us are old enough to have experienced what a blessed glad tidings it was to discover that the Church, this perfect society, is also and above all the living Body of Christ, Christ extended in time, or, to use Cardinal Suhard's happy phrase, "Christ incarnate in each generation." It meant a new and joyful rediscovery of Christianity to realize that the Church is not merely a wonderful machinery of salvation, but our mother, the bride of Christ, in whom and by whom we share in the very life of Christ as His members.

Now my point is that, in regard to the Church, we have got beyond the merely institutional. But we have not yet made the corresponding step in the field of the sacraments. At least we have not in any of our theological manuals, or, to any extent, in our religion textbooks. In our tractate on the sacraments we are still where we were twenty or some years ago in the tractate on the Church.

As in the case of theology on the Church, so also in that on the sacraments our tractate has been developed and crystallized to a large extent by opposition to heresy and especially to the Reformers. Our understanding, and teaching, of the sacraments has been consequently one sided. F. X. Arnold, in an essay of capital importance in *Die Messe in der Glaubensver-kündigung*, pp. 114–164, substantiates this assertion in detail, and shows how it came about after the Council of Trent. As in the tractate on the Church, the institutional instead of the life-aspect of the sacraments has been given emphasis. We spend much of our time on: (1) the institution of the sacraments by Christ (largely apologetical), and, especially, (2) their matter and form—all this plus endless discussions in some of our textbooks about attritionism versus contritionism.

Most important of all, however: because the Reformers rejected the sacramental principle—that matter could be the vehicle of grace—our entire emphasis, then and now, has been on the sacraments as instrumental causes, with a malfocus already discussed. Of course, they *are* instrumental causes; but because of the specific nature of the Protestant denial, we have by reaction tended to stress the "causes" at the expense of the "instrumental." We examine the sacraments *in themselves,* putting them under the microscope of our analytic reason, and do not view them sufficiently in their context, in their living and essential relation to their Principal Minister. We have become accustomed to view them *statically* rather than *functionally*.

Or putting it another way: While insisting, in principle, on the sacraments being instrumental causes, we actually think of them very largely as if they were *secondary* causes.

Perhaps an example will better illustrate my meaning. Let us take that of a sculptor using a chisel as an instrumental cause to make a beautiful statue. The really decisive factors in the process are the efficient and formal causes: the skillful artist and the end product he intends to produce. What we are doing in the tractate on the sacraments amounts to, as it were, concentrating attention on the chisel: what it is made of—iron, with certain alloys, with a sharp edge and a wooden handle—etc., etc. (Is this perhaps another instance of that "Catholic materialism" of which E. I. Watkin writes?) Of course, the sacraments as instrumental causes are unique, in that they are instituted as "signs" from the study of which we can draw more definite conclusions than from the study of a chisel about the effects to be produced. Our theology of the sacraments must always remain basically a "sign" theology. But a sign *points beyond itself;* and sacramental signs indeed point triply: not only to present effects, but also to the past and to the future (as already indicated, and as will be reiterated a few paragraphs further along.) I submit that a study of the institution and matter and form of sacraments, essential though it be, is only *preliminary;* it should serve as a background to the really vital question of the divine teleology of the sacraments, their purposiveness and *function* in the divine scheme of the New Dispensation. This latter, it seems to me, constitutes the *soul* of the tractate on the sacraments.

And when I use the word "function" I mean not merely the character of the sacraments as channels of grace for man. As already indicated, the sacraments elevate man precisely for a liturgical purpose: to equip him for the official worship of God, that is, to enable him to share with Jesus Christ in giving due glory to the Father. "Let everything be theocentric," was Pius XII's dictum "On the Liturgy" (no. 33); we have already cited Cardinal Suhard on this subject and might cite Vonier's *Key to the Doctrine of the Eucharist*, pp. 45–50. We must, therefore, look at sacraments not only from below, but from above: from the standpoint of Christ, who is their principal agent. We must begin with Christ, the first and primal sacrament: otherwise all we have is seven fragments, more or less and somehow correlated.

Christ, the God-Man, is the great sacrament, through the visible sign of His humanity manifesting the divinity, carrying on His highpriestly work of reconciling men to God, of uniting them with Himself in paying due worship to the Father. That highpriestly work of the primal sacrament, then, is continued through time by the Mystic Christ, the Church, herself the *pleroma Christou* (the complementary fullness of Christ), the *sacramentum absconditum a saeculis in Deo*—"the mystery hidden from all ages in God." The Church, one with Christ, is, like Christ, also the great sacrament. She is of her essence the *communio sanctorum*, i.e., the *communio sacramentorum*.[1] She is a sacramental organism, a community of sacraments. Hence the patristic emphasis on the significance of the Church issuing from the pierced side of Christ under the signs of water and blood (baptism and Eucharist).[2]

[1] Cf. *The Catechism of the Council of Trent*: "First of all, the faithful are to be taught that this article ('*communio sanctorum*') is as it were an explanation of the preceding one, on the one, holy, Catholic Church. For the fruits of all the sacraments belong to all the faithful: by the sacraments they are joined and wedded (*connectuntur et copulantur*) to Christ as by sacred bonds. And that by the phrase *communio sanctorum* is to be understood *sacramentorum communio*, the Fathers make clear in the Creed by the following words: *confiteor unum baptisma*" (I, 10, 22).

[2] The new feast of the Sacred Heart in its breviary lessons handily summarizes (and underscores) the rich traditions in the matter. Quoted are St. Augustine, St. John Chrysostom, St. Cyril of Alexandria, St. Bonaventure, St. Bernardine of Siena, and St. Lawrence Justinian. Even the eighteenth-century Vespers hymn gives eloquent witness: *Ex corde scisso Ecclesia Christo iugata nascitur*—"O wounded Heart, whence sprang the Church, the

The Church, therefore, not merely *has* the sacraments, to dispense them: rather, she is *constituted* by sacraments, she lives by sacraments, she grows by sacraments.[3] Her life is sacramental. That is to say, Christ Himself continues His highpriestly work in the Church, by means of the sacraments. *Sacramenta humanitatis*, St. Thomas calls them (*Summa Theologica*, III, q. 80, a. 5). As Christ worked through His humanity, historically, healing, exorcising, sanctifying, so now He acts through this new Body of His, the Church. The sacraments are the continuation of His blessed epiphany among men. Christ yesterday (in the Holy Land), Christ today, Christ forever! (cf. Hebr. 13:8). Christ is the principal agent. He is present and personally *agens*: "Go, baptize . . . and I shall be with you all days." Christ's passion and death as the efficient cause of the grace of the sacraments means precisely that His passion and death are *efficiens*, operative, here and now. It is not a case of *actio in distans*. It is not Paul who baptizes, it is not Peter who baptizes, St. Augustine assures us; it is Christ who baptizes. "Those waters and those words (of baptism), in the last analysis, are poured out by the hand, and are spoken by the mouth of Christ; they are truly His tools, as St. Thomas says so constantly."[4]

In fact, Christ our high priest is operative and active now, in our midst, in a manner more wonderful, more "effective," than when He dwelt bodily on earth. That is why He could say: "It is good for you that I go." Then His disciples walked *with* Christ; now, through the sacraments, we live *in* Christ.

The sacraments, accordingly, are the extension and realization in time of Christ's redeeming activities. This basic conception is obscured by many theological manuals and catechisms, which treat of grace, and then of the sacraments as the principal

---

Saviour's Bride." St. Augustine states the whole idea succinctly: "Christ died that the Church might come into being . . . When Christ died, his side was pierced with a lance, in order that the sacraments might flow forth from which the Church is formed" (*In Joann.*, Tr. 9, n. 10).

[3] *"Ecclesia formaliter et essentialiter constituitur per coenam eucharisticam"* (Dom Anselm Stolz, *Manuale Theologiae Dogmaticae: De Ecclesia*, p. 22).

[4] Vonier, *A Key to the Doctrine of the Eucharist*, p. 30; also pp. 67 ff., and the whole of Chapter 8. Cf. *Mediator Dei*, n. 20.

means of grace. Not so St. Thomas. He outlines the life of Christ: His birth, passion, resurrection, ascension, etc., and then immediately takes up the sacraments, the continuation (not merely application) of those redemptive acts. For, as St. Leo stated in a monumental phrase: "Whatever was visible in the life of Christ has passed over into the sacraments."[5]

We might say, then, that sacraments are not so much something we "receive" (e.g., "He received extreme unction"); rather, we should regard them first of all as activities of Christ, by which He lifts us up into Himself, into the redeemed community, uniting us to His ultimate objective: to praise God. "May God be glorified *in all things*"—and eminently in the sacraments. After all, the very foundation of Christian life, the character of baptism, is already a deputation to cult.

This capital point of Christ's being personally present and principal agent in the sacraments could be further developed. It might seem that the ultimate has been said when we state that Christ present, living in the Church, lifts us up to share in His life and in His work of praise. But the reality seems to be yet greater. In the following chapter, "Initiation into Christian Life and Worship," we shall see at length what St. Cyril of Jerusalem and what the Angelic Doctor have to say about this reality. We may here anticipatorily summarize their teaching on the subject as the view that sacraments achieve their effect by causing us mystically to re-enact Christ's redemptive drama.

The sacraments, then, according to these authorities, mean more than Christ's giving us a share in His life, giving us the grace of adoption. That is the *result* of something prior, something even more basic, something we might call more "ontological." We are saved, not just by the application of Christ's saving grace to us, not just by the extension of His life to us. We are saved, basically, by being baptized, dipped, into the passion and resurrection of Christ. In the sacrament He unites us to the *source* of His saving grace. In the real sense of the word, we are saved *in* Christ's passion and resurrection: in His dying and rising. What happened to our Head, really and physically, now happens to us really though sacramentally. Christ is *agens*, He

[5] *Sermon 75*, 2. Cf. *Mediator Dei*, n. 20, 22, 29.

is present and operative in the sacrament, redeeming us here and now by assimilating us to His death and resurrection, which receive new actuality in us. Christianity is the glad tidings of the fact that Christ's death and resurrection embraces, is communicated to, each successive generation of men, and thus (as a consequence, we might say), enabling them to die to the old man of sin and to live the life of the New Man, Christ Himself.

According to Vonier (*op. cit.*, pp. 19–23), and as we have occasion to remark elsewhere in this book, this reality of Christ in His saving passion and resurrection being present and *operative* in the sacraments, is contained in St. Thomas' description of the threefold significance of every sacrament. (1) As a commemorative sign, it signifies (and effects, makes present and operative) Christ's passion and resurrection. (2) As a sign of the present, it confers sacramental grace. (3) As a prognostic sign it is the pledge and anticipation of eternal glory. "Christ yesterday, today, and forever." Need it be pointed out that we have ordinarily contented ourselves with explaining the present significance: the specific grace conferred?

This broader, more Christ-centered view of the sacraments enables us to have a more *unified* understanding of them. They are not merely seven segments or chapters of our spiritual life. Rather, Christ's passion and resurrection is made present in its fullness in the Holy Eucharist—the sum and center of the sacramental dispensation. The other sacraments are, as it were, echoes, or "images" of the Eucharist, which is the sacrament *par excellence*. "The Eucharist is the fountainhead, while all the other sacraments are the rivulets," says the Catechism of the Council of Trent (n. 228).[6] In these other sacraments, then, the passion and resurrection of Christ become operative *for specific ends*, all of them, however, related essentially to the Eucharist, their summation and source. Baptism and confirmation lead to (and penance restores to) the Eucharist; holy orders and matrimony, each in its proper manner, are sacraments of service to the Eucharist; and extreme unction is the final flowering of the Eucharist. But in every case, in the Eucharistic sun as well as in its sacrament "planets," the mystery re-presented,

6 Cf. also St. Thomas, *Sent.* 4, d. 8, q. 2, a. 2, q. 2, ad 4; *Summa Theologica*, II, q. 73, a. 4, ad 2; also Chapter 7 of Vonier's *Key*.

which becomes presently operative, is the saving passion and glorious rising of Christ.

That baptism, for example, is such an "image" of the Eucharist, a being dipped into Christ's passion and resurrection, is clear enough from St. Paul, as we shall see in the next chapter. It is not always so clearly evident in the case of the other sacraments. I should like, however, to indicate briefly how it holds true of matrimony and extreme unction, sacraments which may be most puzzling in this regard.

How can matrimony be called an effective sign of Christ's death and resurrection? How is it a "rivulet" of the Eucharistic fountainhead? Christ at the Last Supper said: "This cup *is the new covenant* in my blood" (Luke 22:20). Covenant means treaty, contract. And the scriptural connotation of the word, as is being more clearly recognized by modern scholars, is largely matrimonial, a fact which we shall also develop in the chapter "The Marriage of Christ and the Church." God in the Old Testament is the spouse who entered upon a marriage-covenant with His servant bride, the Jewish people (cf. Gal. 4:31). This bride proved unfaithful; and the perfect espousals between God and mankind were to take place with the advent of the Redeemer. Christ in His passion was the divine spouse who won for Himself a new bride (the Church, the new Eve, issued forth from the open side of Christ, the second Adam). Thus was the new covenant established. And every Mass is a renewal of that marriage-covenant. *Every Mass is a nuptial Mass,* in which Christ's spousal relations with His bride, the Church, receive fresh actuality. Christian matrimony, accordingly, as the sign of Christ's nuptials with His Church (Eph. 6:32), is a miniature of the great exemplar: matrimony has its roots in the Eucharist; it is in its own way a "renewal" of the Eucharistic mystery for the specific compass of the Christian family.

Or let us consider extreme unction when administered to consecrate Christian dying. What happens to us spiritually, and according to the will, in every Eucharist (our union with the sacrificial death of Christ), here finds its *"physical"* realization. Our dying, not as something passive which we have to suffer, but as our positive act, our greatest opportunity, is united to the death of Christ—that death which He also underwent *quia ipse voluit:* "because He willed to die." And so our dying, like His, becomes a *beata passio,* a blessed passion: and that means also, an *unctio ad gloriam,* an anointing unto glory, unto life. Christ makes His death operative in the sacrament of extreme unction, plunges us into His own death, in order that of our dying, too, it may be said: Did you not know that he had to pass through these sufferings, in order thus to enter into his glory?

We must also consider, if briefly, the eschatological, the prognostic significance of the sacraments, particularly in relation to our bodies. There has been a strong tendency to hyperspiritualize our religion, to think of salvation too exclusively in terms of the soul. This is all the more curious, in view of the fact that our religion is incarnational, sacramental. Every sacrament, and more especially *the* sacrament, the Holy Eucharist, already as a sign of the present affects and sanctifies our bodies too. ("Lord, may the working of Thy heavenly gift take hold of us, we pray Thee, body and soul": Postcommunion, Fifteenth Sunday after Pentecost.) And as a prognostic sign, it is a pledge and seed of *bodily* resurrection and immortality. We must work out our salvation in and through our body, which must become a fit companion for the soul in its worship of God; and the sacraments have the major role to perform in that process.

In the preceding chapter we saw something of how the distinction developed historically between sacraments and sacramentals, and how this distinction, though absolutely necessary, led to an isolation of the sacramentals in a kind of no-man's-land of dogmatic theology.

The author's own first insight into the relation of sacramentals to the sacraments came from a reading of St. Hippolytus' *Apostolic Tradition.* Some readers may recall that St. Hippolytus wrote this work about A.D. 200, and for the express purpose of inculcating the liturgical and disciplinary traditions of the Church at Rome. After describing the celebration of the Eucharist, effected by the laying of hands over the gifts and by the great consecratory prayer, St. Hippolytus adds: "If any one offers oil, he (the bishop) shall make eucharist (i.e., render thanks) as at the oblation of bread and wine. But he shall not say word for word (the same prayer) but with similar effect, saying . . ."

The blessing of the oil (a sacramental) is therefore, in its own minor way, an echo of the Eucharist—as the sacraments are its "echo" in a major manner. Christ came to restore *all* things, to bring *all* things to a head in Himself, not just persons. The Christmas Martyrology tells us: "Who by his most loving and merciful coming, wishing *to consecrate the world . . . mundum volens consecrare . . .*" Perhaps it was to teach us this lesson that Christ permitted the saving flood of His precious Blood to flow upon the earth from the cross. This "consecration" of the world, accomplished in the passion and resurrection, is re-enacted in the Eucharist. It is realized for specific ends, in regard to *persons,* in the sacraments; it is realized in regard to both *persons and things,* by means of sacramentals. The sacramentals are thus echoes of the Eucharist, either directly, or mediately, through the other sacraments. But the point at issue is that they belong organically to the same "family" as the sacraments. They are not the "step-sisters" of the sacraments that we have somehow made them; they are at least "half-sisters."

1) Obvious instances of sacramentals that echo the Eucharist *directly* are the consecrations of persons, e.g., of virgins. Seen thus, religious profession is restored to proper perspective. Religious profession has traditionally been compared to baptism: it is a second baptism. Now in baptism the "vows," the renunciations and the positive pledgings of faith and faithfulness, are preparatory; the real baptismal consecration follows. So also in the consecration of a virgin: the vows that the virgin pronounces, pledging herself to God, are preparatory to (and express obligations involved in) her consecration *by God,* contained in the solemn preface. "For you have not chosen Me, but I have chosen you."

Also the blessing or consecration of things is often a direct reflection, irradiation, of the cosmic *consecratio mundi* effected by the Eucharist. Such blessings are even sometimes externally similar to the Eucharistic anaphora, by reason of a great "eucharistic" or preface-like prayer of consecration: e.g., the blessing of Easter water and Easter candle, of chrism, and of altars. In the blessing of palms this echoing of the Eucharist is perhaps most striking: there is an introit, collect, lesson, gradual, gospel ("Mass of the Catechumens"), followed by the consecrating preface (the anaphora or canon). Nor is it irrelevant to our thesis that many of the important blessings take place during or in conjunction with Holy Mass.

The same thought, of Christ's passion and resurrection extending ever farther outward from the fountainhead of the Eucharist, and enveloping the whole world in its consecrating and saving efficacy, is brought home by the fact that at the Pasch, the Holy Week celebrating Christ's passage from death to life, all essentials for man's living are blessed: water, oil, fire, light, food (especially meat, eggs, and bread), and houses.

And as a Benedictine, the author would like to call attention to the manner in which St. Benedict constantly associates the common meal, blessed by prayer, with the *opus Dei* and the Eucharist. For St. Benedict, eating together is an important spiritual exercise, a grace-giving imitation of the Last Supper.

In a class apart, by virtue of its eminence, stands the sacramental of the Divine Office. It hardly needs to be explained in detail how it directly reflects the Eucharist, how its hours are so many planets carrying the light of Eucharistic worship into the various parts of the day and night.

2) Instances of sacramentals echoing the Eucharist *mediately,* through the other sacraments, are the various sacramentals grouped around baptism, penance, matrimony, extreme unction, etc. Already Hippolytus speaks of the sign of the cross as an "image of baptism" (ch. 37, 2). And how we have failed to pay due justice to the cleansing and sanctifying power of that other image of baptism, holy water! After the officiant's solemn "May the power of the Holy Spirit descend into this brimming font," that water—*ex opere operantis Ecclesiae*—has spiritual efficacy, or else the Church is misleading us by a solemn play-acting unworthy of her. Blessed water is a small rivulet, deriving from the stream of baptism, as this in turn flows forth from the fountainhead of the altar.

In this way, I believe, we are able to achieve a unified view of the sacraments and sacramentals. The latter are organically grouped around the sacraments and around *the* sacrament, as their irradiations into every corner of human life and of the cosmos.

Recall, for instance, how the sacramentals consecrate space and time.

The basic consecration of *space* takes place in the consecration of a church. The texts of the dedication of a church, in missal and breviary, are eloquent. The church building, the space enclosing the consecrated altar of sacrifice, is heaven on earth. "Awe-inspiring is this place: this is the house of God and gate of heaven, and it shall be called the palace of God." Quite apart from the Reserved Species, this is the "house of God," "My house"; it is the holy city, the new Jerusalem come upon earth. "The church building does not become holy by the fact that holy persons pray and worship in it: *we* do not make the church holy; it is filled with the divine presence and makes us holy."[7] St. Thomas says, in fact, that very likely a man by entering a consecrated church receives the remission of his venial sins, just as he does by sprinkling with holy water (*Summa Theologica*, III, q. 83, a. 3, ad 3).

But the church building, "built of living stones" (Vespers, hymn of dedication), is a symbol of the living Church which is the parish. Hence the consecration of a parish church amounts to a dedication to God of the entire parish, in all its territorial extent. This dedication becomes more explicit in various special blessings: of the home and its rooms, of barns and granaries, of fields, meadows, vineyards, archives, school, library, printing shop, etc. The consecration of space reaches out from the altar, from the church, to embrace all other areas, all places in which men live and labor, so that all human life and effort may become more directly and consciously part of the great act of sacrificial worship.

The consecration of *time* likewise derives from the altar. For the liturgical year, the week and the day are nothing else than the more or less extensive framework of the eucharistic sacrifice, a fact which the August 1960, revision of the calendar brings vividly to mind. Here too we can say: it is not we who make time holy, but time, in which the life and work of Christ unfolds, sanctifies us. Every day by the providence of God is the

[7] Pinsk, *Die Sakramentale Welt*, p. 128.

acceptable time, the day of salvation. For every day, at its minimum, is a *feria*, a festal day, a holyday: for it is a day of Eucharistic celebration. We shall have more to say of the liturgical year, of course, in the chapter "The Church Year in Action."

Perhaps even more important than all the explanation just given is the idea that, as with the sacraments, so also in the case of the sacramentals, we should think of them in terms of the extended activities of *Christ*. We speak of them, it is true, as being effective *ex opere operantis Ecclesiae*. But the Church cannot be thought of apart from Christ, independently of Christ. She is His bride, carrying on His work in His name, in His person. Pius XII, in *Mediator Dei*, it will be recalled from the preceding chapter, does not make distinctions between sacraments and sacramentals when he speaks of the liturgy as being the continuation of the priestly work of Christ.

Christ is the pantocrator, the consecrator of the world. It is the redemptive power of Christ, it is Christ the high priest, who is operative when the Church prays that the world be blessed.

Finally, we may draw yet one more comparison between the sacramentals and sacraments. I said earlier that in the sacraments man is not the ultimate terminus. Rather, Christ by His sacraments reaches out and lifts man into Himself, into the current of His life, that man in Christ may glorify God more worthily. Similarly with the sacramentals. We sometimes imagine the divine blessing as a sort of heavenly, beneficent dew descending on creation. Thus created things become, in our thinking, the terminus of the process. But again, this presents only a partial understanding of the story. We must also, and above all, think of sacramentals as part of the process by which Christ recapitulates *all* things in Himself, so that creation, which was groaning and in travail, waiting for the redemption to come, now can again sing its praises of God properly—and even better than before the Fall, for now it can become a vehicle of divine life! In respect of the Fall's effect on the *cosmos*, too, we can sing: "O happy fault!"

Blessing, *benedictio*, does not merely mean, then, God's blessing of things. It can and does mean likewise that things bless God: *Benedicite omnia opera Domini Dominum: laudate et superexaltate eum in saecula*—"Bless the Lord all ye works of the Lord: praise and exalt him above all forever."

III. INITIATION INTO CHRISTIAN LIFE AND WORSHIP

Very recently I read in a Catholic periodical that the sacrament of baptism is again coming into its own; that it is no longer being considered so exclusively from the negative aspect, as a forgiveness of original and actual sin, but that its positive aspect is again being given the prominence that is its due; that we are again learning to appreciate how the individual, through baptism, is made a son of God and heir of heaven; that we are again becoming aware more keenly of the life of sanctifying grace which the baptized receives. We should be grateful for the advance which this signifies over the previous more negative treatment, but I believe that, to be just to the full positive significance of baptism, we must with Saint Paul go yet a step further. First of all, the sacrament of baptism is not the mere *application* of Christ's divine life to the individual, like adding spiritual frosting to the cake of human nature, if this be not too flippant a comparison. Rather, what we said summarily in the preceding chapter about St. Cyril's and Aquinas's teaching on the mystical *rôle* in which the sacraments cast us must now be applied fully to baptism.

Saint Paul tells us in his Epistle to the Romans: "We were baptized (i.e. *plunged*) into Christ Jesus." Saint Paul has in mind the ancient form of administering baptism through immersion. As the candidate is "immerged," dipped entirely into water, so is he spiritually immersed into Christ, becomes Christified (if I may coin the word).

Liturgical Week 1940, Chicago.

We have the beautiful English word "christened" to describe baptism. No other language has so apt a word for it. Through baptism we are christened, become Christed, become one with Christ; we are no longer mere human beings with merely the added obligation of now imitating Christ, and, certain of the graces of Christ, to fulfill our function. No, we are christened, we have become something completely new. We are now "a new creature in Christ," a new creation. Christ's life has become our life; we live now, not we, but Christ in us.

Baptism, therefore, has not merely the effect of cleansing us from sin, and of giving us the grace of adoption, but is first of all a plunging of our entire being into Christ. His redemptive death and resurrection becomes *ours*, and it is because we are baptized, that is, plunged into His death (as Saint Paul tells us) that we die to sin; and it is because we are baptized into His resurrection that His glorious life becomes ours.

I say this is important to keep clearly in mind. Baptism is not merely the *application* of Christ's merits and graces to us, but is our complete immerging into Christ, into His saving death, into His life-giving resurrection. To quote Saint Paul: "For we are buried together with Him by baptism into death; that as Christ is risen from the dead by the glory of the Father, so we also may walk in newness of life."

This basic significance of baptism is clearly expressed by Saint Cyril of Jerusalem in his famous catechetical lectures. His evidence is all the stronger, in that it was precisely for these catechetical lectures, in which he instructs candidates for baptism, that Saint Cyril was made a doctor of the Church. "Let no one then suppose that baptism is merely the grace of remission of sins, or merely that of adoption. . . . Paul cries aloud and says: 'Know ye not that as many of us as were baptized into Christ Jesus were baptized into His death? Therefore we are buried with Him by baptism into death.' These words Saint Paul spoke to them who had settled with themselves that baptism ministers to us the remission of sins, and adoption, but not that further it has communion also, in re-presentation, with Christ's true sufferings. In order, therefore, that we may learn that whatsoever things Christ endured, He suffered them for us and our salvation, and that *in reality, not in appearance*, we also are made partakers of His sufferings, Paul cried out with all exactness of truth: 'For if we have been planted together in the likeness of His death, we shall be also in the likeness of His resurrection.'

"As Christ was in truth crucified and buried and raised; you also are in likeness in baptism accounted worthy of being crucified, buried and raised together with Him" (XX, 6, 7; XXI, 2).

So the first thing, the most important thing, is this baptism into Christ, into His death and resurrection; and as a consequence of this union with Christ we are cleansed from sin.

Or, as Saint Thomas later tells us: "Through baptism man is incorporated into the passion and death of Christ; wherefrom it follows that the passion (not merely its effects) is communicated to the baptized person as if he himself had suffered and died" (*Sum. Theol.*, III, q. 66, ad 9).

It is for this reason, namely, that baptism is not merely the application of Christ's merits and graces but an immerging into His death and resurrection, that the Church has from earliest times chosen Easter, the day of Christ's greatest redemptive work, as the special day for Christian baptism.

As Tertullian tells us, "A solemn day for baptism is Easter (*Pascha*), for at this time the passion of Christ, into which we were baptized, took place" (*De Baptismo*, 19).

That is the first point.

Secondly, since baptism is of its nature a plunging into Christ, it follows that baptism is of its very nature also an immerging into the *whole* Christ, head and body. It is not so much the union of the individual with Christ directly, but rather through the medium of the Church, Christ's body. In other words, baptism has essentially a social significance; and this is the second principal point I want to make concerning the meaning of baptism.

Now, it has been customary for several centuries to divide the sacraments into two classes. Those which are for the perfection of the individual: baptism, confirmation, penance, Eucharist, and extreme unction. And those which are principally for the perfection of the social body: matrimony and holy orders.

This division is derived, according to the letter of it at least, from Saint Thomas, who got it from Hugh of Saint Victor;

and because it is a nice, simple division, it has been continuously accepted and thoroughly overworked, exaggerated beyond anything that Saint Thomas had in mind. True, some sacraments have more social significance than others, and although he classifies baptism as among those sacraments which are for the perfection of the individual, Saint Thomas shows by his entire treatment of this sacrament that he does not dream of neglecting its social significance, as has been done to such a large extent subsequently.

On the contrary, his keen awareness of what Saint Paul calls "baptism into Christ's body" makes Saint Thomas also emphasize this point. He obviously based the distinction of sacraments for the individual and sacraments for the social body on the parallelism that exists between the natural and the supernatural life. Thus, baptism, the new birth in Christ, corresponds to the natural birth of the infant, and while it is true that birth primarily concerns the individual that is born, I think we need but ask the parents of any newborn child whether this birth does not also very deeply and intimately concern them and the entire family. The point need hardly be demonstrated.

We may, however, go a step further. Liturgists generally have made it clear that the Church becomes concrete in the parish; that the parish, the pastor and the community of parishioners *are* the Church, Christ's Body in miniature, but in true reality. So if baptism means a birth into the Church, it means more immediately a birth into a particular church, into a definite mystical body in miniature. That is to say, every baptism of a new member of the parish very intimately concerns the whole parish, every single member of the parish. We may say it is a "blessed event" for the whole family of God represented by that particular parish.

It is not surprising, therefore, that the same Saint Paul who speaks so eloquently of "baptizing into Christ" speaks just as eloquently of baptizing into one body; and in saying these words, he is addressing a definite community, and for the precise purpose of restoring peace and harmony, of restoring their sense of mutual responsibility.

Again he says: "All you who are baptized into Christ, have put on Christ. . . . You are all one in Christ Jesus." This was also spoken to a particular congregation to encourage mutual charity.

The history of the early Church, moreover, informs us how much of a parish event each baptism was considered, how keenly the members of the parish felt their responsibility toward the candidate for baptism, and toward the newly baptized. In what is ordinarily considered the earliest Christian document outside of the New Testament, in the *Teaching of the Twelve Apostles,* written about the year 90, we have the following: "And before the baptism, let the baptizer and him who is to be baptized fast, and all others who are able" (VII, 4).

Similarly Saint Justin, writing about the year 150, says concerning the preparation for baptism: "As many as are persuaded and believe that what we teach is true . . . are instructed to pray and to entreat God with fasting . . . *we praying and fasting with them*" (I Apology, LXI).

Now this ancient practice of the community praying and fasting with the candidate for baptism became stabilized soon after, in the discipline of the Lenten season. Lent was not merely, or even principally, a time in which the Christian community did penance for its sins. It was rather a time in which the members of the parish family of God showed their fraternal, spiritual interest in the prospective new members of their family.

The Mass of the Catechumens during Lent could well have been called the Mass *for* the Catechumens, as is evident even in our Missal today, where most of the epistles and gospels are obviously intended for the instruction of the baptismal candidate. In fact, we might compare Lent to the novitiate of a religious community. Not only the novice master, but the entire community keeps its eyes on the novices and assists them, especially through prayer.

So also the entire Christian community took an interest in the catechumens, helped them with prayer, and sat in judgment on their worthiness. There were three official "scrutinies," or public examinations of the candidates, during Lent, to which all the parish was invited. The names of the candidates were openly announced, and objections could be voiced.

But, some of us may think, these are ancient practices. How do they concern us today?

It is true that the baptism of adults, with its lengthy ceremonial which these ancient practices presuppose, is nowadays rather exceptional. But the idea behind these practices, the vital meaning of baptism for the whole parish, is as actual today as it was then.

Every baptism is a feast of joy at which the parochial family could well sing what the Church sings at Christmas: *"Puer natus est nobis—A child is born to us, and a son is given to us."*

Moreover, we still have the season of Lent to which we might well restore some of its baptismal significance, not only praying for all new members of the parish but also preparing ourselves for the renewal of our own baptismal grace at Easter.

Then, too, let us not forget that the meaning of baptism remains the same in the twentieth as in the second century; that, accordingly, the parish significance of this sacrament is urged just as strongly by the Church legislation today as it was in those earlier centuries, even though some liturgical practices may have changed in the course of time. Today, also, the administration of solemn baptism and the important rite of blessing the baptismal font on Holy Saturday is the personal privilege and duty of the pastor, the father of the parochial family.

Today, as well as in former centuries, the font, which Pseudo-Denys of old called "the maternal womb (of the Church) in which children are assumed," is for the parish community the most sacred place after the altar and the tabernacle. It is in reality the sacred womb of our mother, the Church, which, having been made fruitful by the holy oil of chrism, bears children to Christ, and brothers and sisters to all members of the parish family. Accordingly, the font is normally allowed only in the parish church, the spouse of Christ.

Every administration of baptism is a parochial event, second in importance only to the community sacrifice of the Mass. There are parishes which celebrate baptism as a part of, or even exclusively as, the Sunday afternoon service. The time for baptism is announced at the Sunday Masses and the parishioners are invited to participate in the service. The most common form of such participation consists, at least in the beginning, of a second priest explaining the rite as it progresses, and of all present renewing their own baptismal vows after the child has been baptized.

Another very simple but meaningful manner of participation is for the congregation to join in the Creed and the Our Father which the rubrics prescribe for priest and sponsors. For the sponsors not only represent the child (adults have sponsors too) but are representatives of the community of the faithful, going bond, as it were, for this new member of the community.

Hence if the congregation recites the Creed and the Our Father, they do so not merely as a remembrance and a renewal of their own baptism, but as an expression of their will to assist this new member to lead a good Christian life; to be true to the Creed, and to live as a true son of "Our Father."

It is well to remember that the Creed and the Our Father are in a special manner baptismal prayers. They were not taught to the catechumen, the candidate for baptism, until shortly before he was to receive the sacrament. The Creed was not merely an expression of assent to the truths of faith; it was a pledge of loyalty to the triune God and to the *Ecclesia Sancta,* the community of saints into which he was being introduced.

Three times he renounced Satan, his works and all his pomps. And correspondingly, three times he swore his oath of allegiance, his *Credo;* to God the Father, to God the Son; to God the Holy Ghost and the Holy Church.

The Creed was therefore an oath of allegiance, the new member's oath of loyalty. And so important was this *Credo,* this oath, considered, that Tertullian calls baptism a *sacramentum,* that is, an oath, comparing it with the oath that soldiers swore to the Emperor.

When the congregation, therefore, prays the Creed with the candidate or with the sponsors, they renew their own oath of allegiance, and also pledge their support to this new member of the spiritual family, to help him in being true to his solemn promise.

Similarly, the Our Father is specifically a baptismal prayer. It has always been considered as the exclusive privilege of the baptized Christian, living in community with the Church. Only the baptized has the full right to address God as Father, for only he is truly born of God and is truly the brother of the only begotten Son of the Father. Nor can a sectarian have the full right to say Our Father, because he is not a member of the community of the sons of God, the Church.

Accordingly, when the congregation prays the "Our Father," now for the first time with their new fellow member, it is a welcome into the parish, this family of God, a welcome to their new brother.

Again, it is a promise to treat him as a true brother, to "forgive as we forgive"; it is a pledge to live in love and harmony with him, unto the mutual edification (building up) of the Body of Christ in this parish.

And even if this solemn recitation of the Creed and the Our Father with the candidate for baptism is not carried out, all who are present at the ceremony, and even all who are absent, can at least silently pray these two baptismal prayers, conscious that they are promising to assist their new brother in Christ on his way to salvation.

In parishes where baptism is conferred on Sundays, the pastor might recommend that parishioners add the Creed and the Our Father to their evening prayers with this intention. Or better still, he might, after due explanation, ask his parishioners to pray the Creed and the Our Father at Sunday Mass with this intention.

Thus a seemingly insignificant ceremony of the baptismal rite can become an effective means of nourishing parish consciousness and the sense of mutual fraternal responsibility.

In this connection also, we may point out the rather striking fact that just these two baptismal prayers, the Creed and the Our Father, are given such a prominent position in the most important function of every Christian and of the parish, that is, in the holy sacrifice of the Mass. Furthermore both are in the Mass as distinctly community prayers.

The Creed is the solemn song of the baptized members of this family of God, who together renew their allegiance to God before beginning the sacrificial action. It would be a wonderful thing if this congregational singing of the Creed soon becomes a common practice. I remember attending a High Mass in Westminster Cathedral some years ago. The choir performed beautifully, and I was duly edified; but then came the Creed, and the entire vast congregation joined in with a will and almost raised the roof. It nearly swept me off my feet, all the more so since it was unexpected.

In an age of unbelief, this family of God solemnly professed their faith, solemnly renewed their baptismal pledge of fidelity to God and His Church, joyously sang their determination to strive together as the Body of Christ, to fight for His kingdom. And they knew that it was in that Holy Sacrifice which they were about to begin that was stored the strength by which they could win that fight.

This Creed, this simple baptismal song and oath of loyalty, is a powerful thing. Other groups have their "Marseillaise," "God Save the King," and "God Bless America." We also, the family of the baptized, the family of God's children, have our song by which to pledge anew our faith, our joyous loyalty. It would be a good thing if all of us knew it, if we would sing it at public and especially at parish gatherings, at solemn occasions.

Then there is our second baptismal prayer, the Our Father. With this most beautiful of all prayers, the prayer of the children of God made such through baptism, we together begin more immediately to prepare ourselves for receiving the divine food which, as Saint Thomas tells us, has for its effect to unite us more closely to each other in Christ.

In every Mass, this Our Father should remind us of our mutual consecration into the body of Christ at baptism, of the mutual charity with which, together with our brethren, we approach the sacrament of still greater union. And thus baptism, and the prayers of baptism, lead us to the Holy Eucharist, sacrifice and sacrament which is the summit of the liturgical (i.e., the normal) spiritual life, and to which, as Saint Thomas reminds us, baptism is by its nature ordered, as completion.

IV. REBIRTH IN CHRIST

Cardinal Cushing once remarked that Pius XII might well be called the pope of holy baptism. For his restoration of the Easter Vigil with its solemn renewal of the baptismal vows in English, his permission to us in the U.S. to administer baptism in English, and especially his great encyclicals on the Mystical Body and on worship are striking evidence that Pope Pius XII was "anxious that the people have an understanding and a love for holy baptism."

Our age has often been called the age of the Mystical Body. As Romano Guardini has phrased it in a famous sentence: "Ours is the age in which the Church is coming to life in the hearts of men." That entails, firstly and most basically, that ours is the age in which, through the inspired guidance of the Holy Spirit, Catholics are becoming newly aware of the fuller meaning of the sacrament of baptism whereby we become members of the Mystical Body. In other words, a sound and lively baptismal consciousness is a prerequisite, not only to the liturgical apostolate, but also to the other splendid Catholic apostolates that happily characterize our age of the Mystical Body.

But how can our people acquire this lively awareness of their dignity and vocation as baptized members of Christ, as sons of God and brothers of Christ, brothers, too, of all members of Christ's Body? How can they acquire such a vital awareness that it will be the decisive and permanent inspiration of a wholly Christian life, both personal and social?

A retreat master in our monastery many years ago—so many that I have even forgotten who it was—used an approach which I thought very effective and which, therefore, with his presumed permission, I would like to share with my readers.

I have often wished (he said) that I could have lived at the time of Christ; for many reasons. One of them is that I wish I could have asked St. Peter shortly before the Last Supper: "Tell me, Peter, what does it mean to you to be a disciple of Christ?" No doubt St. Peter, the good, gruff St. Peter, the strong and childlike St. Peter, would have looked important; for he already knew that he was first in that group of apostles. And perhaps he would have hemmed and hawed a few times for effect. Then he would very likely have told me that being a disciple of Christ means loyalty to Christ, means following Christ through all difficulties, trying to imitate His example, obeying His commands, loving Him and being loved by Him.

And then I would like to have asked that same St. Peter after the Last Supper. What a different answer it would have been! Perhaps St. Peter would not have been able to answer at all. His great heart would have been so full to overflowing with the things that he had just seen and heard, that he would not have trusted his tongue to give utterance. He who was never at a loss for an answer would have been overwhelmed and perhaps, as after his denial, he would have wept. But they would have been tears of wonderment and gratitude, humble tears of unspeakable awe, at realizing now, *for the first time,* what it really means to be disciple of Christ. Or perhaps this big, rough-spoken man would have stammered, as he stammered in his First Epistle years later, when speaking about baptism: "I have tasted that the Lord is gracious. Crave like newborn babes the spiritual milk."

We should try to imagine to ourselves what Christ's words must have meant to the apostles at the Last Supper. They had been close to Christ for three years, as intimate as man can be to man, or rather, since they now knew that He was the Son of God, as intimate as man can possibly be to God. So they thought. And then at the Last Supper, Christ for the first time opens His heart to them and tells them: "I am the Vine, you are the branches."

We, all of us, have heard that phrase dozens of times. But let us try to visualize its impact on the apostles. The apostles were good, faithful Jews; and for the Jews God was the transcendent God, the Infinitely Other God. It was a great revelation that God the Father vouchsafed to Peter, shortly before, enabling him to recognize Jesus as the true Son of God. And now to be told that this Son of God was actually sharing His divine life with them!

The mystery of the incarnation, of God becoming man, is obviously a tremendous mystery. And yet the mystery of God's being able to raise mere creatures to become the sons of God, sharing in the very life of God, may strike Christians personally as an even greater mystery.

After the Last Supper's discourse, the apostles could think and write and speak of nothing else. This was it! This was the New Testament. This was the glad tidings. When we read the beginning of St. John's First Epistle, written many years later, we still seem to feel the tremulousness of St. John writing: "That which we have seen and heard we announce to you also, in order that you may have fellowship with us (that you may share this gift with us), and that our fellowship may be with the Father and with his Son, Jesus Christ. And we write these things in order that your joy may be full. . . . Behold what manner of charity the Father hath bestowed upon us: that we should be called, *and are,* the Sons of God."

St. Paul, too. His fourteen epistles are nothing else than so many paraphrases of this same identical thought. Scholars tell us that all fourteen of them could be summarized in one short phrase: "in Christ." St. Paul was thoroughly familiar with the Greek language, whose vocabulary has rich nuances of meaning. And yet it was not expressive enough for St. Paul to describe the closeness of our union with Christ; he had to coin new combinations of words to express this inexpressible good news.

And the great St. Augustine. His tomes, likewise, could practically be summarized in the selfsame phrase: "in Christ." Some readers may be familiar with the following passage from his writings: "Let us congratulate ourselves, let us break forth into thanksgiving. We are become not only Christians but Christ. Do we understand, my brethren, the outpouring of God's grace upon us? Let us wonder and shout with gladness: we are become Christ: He is the Head, we are the members."

St. Augustine lived at the time of the so-called christological controversies, which raged particularly in the East; these were controversies about the natures and person of Christ. He knew that these controversies threatened the very existence of the faith in the East, and appreciated the absolute necessity of exact terminology. Yet, at the risk of being seriously misunderstood, he did not hesitate to use a phrase which, taken literally, is certainly wrong. He spoke of our being as it were "one person" with Christ. Surely we are not hypostatically united to Divinity; nevertheless, St. Augustine states that we are, as it were, one person with Christ in order thereby to indicate the intimacy of our union of life with Christ. He used the word "person" because there is none other in the whole realm of human experience that could so adequately express this intimacy.

Because of this *essential* content of the new dispensation, because the gospel is the glad tidings of our life-union with Christ through baptism, we are exhorted by St. Paul: "Rejoice in the Lord always. Again I say, rejoice." He, and St. John, and the others tell us again and again in these or equivalent terms: "Make melody in your hearts."

Christianity is not merely a manner of life or of action, much less is it merely a *Weltanschauung,* a philosophy of life. Christianity is a mystery—a *mysterium*. It is the mystery of Christ's incarnation extending through time, that is, of Christ, the God-Man, active here and now, lifting us unto Himself.

Perhaps the author of this book could explain this somewhat more effectively if allowed to become very personal in the remarks which follow:

There is among our Catholic laity an instinctive reverence for the priesthood, and properly so. If they were asked why they have this high esteem for the priesthood, I think the more thoughtful among them might come up with some such answer as this: "The priest deserves special honor, because he has this special *vocation* from God, because God has chosen him from among all others to carry on His own great work. He has been *consecrated,* set aside, by God for the purpose of God."

Permit me, now, to become quite personal. I have been a priest twenty-four years, and I believe that rarely has there been a day in that span of time when in some way or other I haven't been made conscious of the fact of this *vocation*. I have been a teacher in a boys' college for more than twenty years, and never has a year passed that I did not have a moral certainty in my own mind that many a boy sitting in front of me in my class would have made a much better priest than I, *if* God had chosen him. That is not false humility; that is ordinary common sense. The reason God chose me, consecrated me, can only be the reason of God's mercy, of God's predilection. Certainly it was no merit on my part. And if there is one motivation that should urge me to lead at least a minimum good, holy, priestly life, it is this awareness that God has chosen me. The laity too, expect their priests to try to lead a holy life, and rightly so, for they know that priests have been *called* and *consecrated* by God to carry on His all-important work.

Have we not, however, limited this powerful motivation to holiness too exclusively to priests? When St. Paul speaks of vocation, when he exults in the fact of being elect, of being called, of being chosen, he is not speaking about his priestly dignity. He is speaking about the basic vocation of being called to be members of Christ. And actually, there is less difference (though the difference, obviously, is great) between one in holy orders and a lay member of Christ, than there is between such a member of Christ and those who have not been given this grace. In other words, the idea of *vocation* and of *consecration* is something we priests have no right to keep to ourselves. It is a rightful heritage of each member of the Body of Christ: a motivation which could and should be a powerful incentive to holiness.

The Catholic laity, too, have been called by a great and wonderful *vocation*. There are few, I am sure, who would care to deny that there are millions, and tens of millions, and perhaps hundreds of millions, of pagans who would be much better Catholics than they, *if* God had chosen them: and some, and perhaps many of them, lead better lives than we, despite the abundance of sacramental means at our disposal. All of us, every member of Christ, has been called, has been set aside by God for His purposes. From all eternity God has, as it were, laid His hand on the head of each one of us, and in baptism has *consecrated* us to do His work and to bear His fruit. We are not our own. We cannot use our time and talents merely as we ourselves please. We belong to God—who has actually deigned to make the redemption of the world dependent upon our collaboration!

That realization belongs to every Christian. And that is what we mean when we speak of the need of the renewal of baptismal consciousness. St. Paul told Timothy, "Stir up the grace that is in you by the laying on of hands." He could similarly have said to each of us: "Stir up the grace that is in you by the sacrament of baptism."

And yet, if Catholic laity were asked, "What does it mean to be a disciple of Christ?" I wonder what answer they would give. Again permit me to cite my own experience. I have been a college teacher of religion for more than twenty years. I have not had the advantage of much pastoral work; but in college one is apt to get a fair cross-section from various parts of the country. My observation has been that even among those who have had the advantage of eight years of parochial grade school training and four years of Catholic high school, the majority, to all intents and purposes, seem almost to be still living in the Old Testament. Christianity to their minds seems to be chiefly a surer grasp of divine truths and a higher type of ethics: an obedience to the Ten Commandments which God will reward. In addition, they know of course that obeying the Ten Commandments is helped by "grace." But few among them have a grasp, much less a vital grasp, of what St. Paul in all his epistles was trying to tell us: that now we are a *nova creatura*—a new creature, that we have been re-created, that we have been Christed. Or, as the daily Offertory prayer says, that "we have fellowship in the Godhead of Him who deigned to share our manhood." Few among them seem to realize that in baptism something happened to them analogous to what happens at the Consecration of Mass: that the appearance, the "species," of mere man remained, but that in very truth they have become sons of God.

To bring home to ourselves the meaning of baptism and of sanctifying grace, we must, I believe, *personalize* the concept of grace. Christopher Dawson in one of his writings has summarized the respective views of the Christian East and West by saying that in the East grace has traditionally been described in terms of the in-dwelling of God: of God, the Light, radiating His light into us; whereas in the West, particularly in the past half-dozen or so centuries, there has been a greater emphasis on grace being a "created quality," superadded to man by God. Surely it is that. But have we sufficiently realized the purpose and the effect of that quality given to us: namely, that thereby we become sharers in divine nature? Even the phrase "sanctifying grace" has largely become stripped of spiritual impact. It is something that God gives us to help us lead virtuous lives. If we investigate their meaning, the words do have inspiring content. "Grace" means a gift; "sanctifying" means making holy, i.e., making divine, for only God is holy. "Sanctifying grace," therefore, means God's gift to us, which makes us sharers in His life.

And yet Christ at the Last Supper used different language. He said: "If any man love Me, *We* shall come to make Our abode with him." Christ spoke of grace, of our sonship of God, in terms of the in-dwelling of the divine *Persons* in our souls, that is, in terms of our sharing in the life of the Trinity. Becoming sons of God does not merely mean having divine life. It means sharing in the Triune life, in the infinitely rich life of the Trinity. God dwells in us, but this in-dwelling is not intended to be passive on His part. God by His very nature is pure Act. God desires to be active in us. He wants to radiate Himself. And this radiation of His light and life is grace.

Hence St. Cyril of Alexandria uses the comparison of a piece of iron put into the fire; the iron retains its own nature, but absorbs the heat of the fire and takes on, as it were, the qualities of the fire itself. So too our human nature is transformed by the divine Light dwelling in us. Scheeben, the great theologian of the last century, particularly liked this comparison and made it central in his teaching about grace. I believe we could convincingly speak of our sharing in the life of God, therefore, as a "transfiguration," graphically applying the Scripture story of Christ's own transfiguration on Thabor. The whole process of grace and of growing in grace means a transfiguration effected by God the Light dwelling in us and "enlightening" us.

But God is *Triune*. St. Augustine, who spent fifteen years meditating the mystery of the Trinity, tells us that it is not only the first and greatest mystery, but, precisely because it is the first and greatest, is also the most fruitful mystery for our spiritual life. And in his famous work, *De Trinitate*, he gives us wonderful insights into what our sharing in the life of the Triune God involves.

The One God revealed Himself as Father, Son, and Holy Spirit, not merely to exercise the wits of theologians, to enable them to speak about subsistent relations or (as someone has rather flippantly remarked) to indulge in sacred mathematics. Certainly these things are not unimportant; they are gravely important. But He revealed Himself as Triune in order above all that we might, by knowing Him better, love Him more, and therefore more perfectly realize in our own living the "image" of this Triune life of God which is ours by the grace of baptism.

When we call God "Father," we do not do so as the people of the Old Testament. By faith we humbly but jubilantly acknowledge that the same God the Father who broke the silence at the baptism of Christ and at His transfiguration, saying: "This is My Beloved Son," now says of each one of us: "Truly, this is My beloved son." We are not merely called, but *are*, His sons: not by nature, but by adoption: yet truly His sons. And therefore *audemus dicere*, we dare to say, "Our Father who art in heaven." Because we call Him "Father," it is pitifully inadequate to view Christian life as a sort of ladder which we must climb by our good works in order finally to achieve heaven. Christian life is a gift. We have not first loved God; God has first loved us. By the sacrament of baptism, He has raised us to the divine level. We do not start from below, from the earth's level, and laboriously try somehow to achieve heaven above. God, by His gift, *starts* us, as it were, in heaven, for by grace we share the life of God, we are citizens of heaven, already essentially enjoying the heavenly life. And therefore our efforts at virtue consist above all in putting away the human hindrances, and allowing the divine life to flower and fruit in us. A comparison will illustrate.

If a carpenter constructs a table, the net result—the table—will depend almost entirely on his skill as a carpenter. It is quite different in the case of a farmer or a gardener "producing" a crop. He knows that no matter how hard he works, the good harvest depends ultimately on the life that is in the seed.

Christian life and morality, therefore, are first of all a matter of *being* rather than of becoming. *"Agere sequitur esse: action follows* being." St. Paul said, "Walk worthy of the calling with which you have been called." Walk worthy of the baptism by which Christ lives and wishes to act in you.

This emphasis implies, moreover, that the life of virtue is not something which we can choose to carry out leisurely at our own pace—sometimes, perhaps, even thinking that we are conferring a favor upon God if we perform certain acts. It is not something that we may rightfully choose to do or not to do, just as long as we manage to slip into heaven (as the saying goes) by the skin of our teeth. No; it is a divine urgency in us; it is a life that demands growth; a divine urgency that may not be denied except at the risk of total loss. Let us remember the parable of the one talent.

Putting it very simply: Christianity is a gift: God's gift of divine life. And that *gift becomes an obligation*—our life of virtue. St. Paul repeatedly teaches us this lesson. No one will gainsay that he moralized much; and yet he consistently bases his moralizing on the motivation of our graced being and divine dignity. Ephesians, chapter 5, furnishes an eloquent example: "Be you, therefore, imitators of God *as most dear children . . .* Avoid sin, avoid fornication, let it not so much as be named among you, *as becomes saints . . .* Walk, then, *as children of light."*

Hence St. Paul's insistence on joy, and the whole climate of joy that pervades the New Testament. Somebody who took the trouble to count the passages has stated that the exhortation "rejoice," or its equivalent, is found more than three hundred times in Holy Scripture. Even in the Old Testament; but far more insistently in the New Testament. The wellsprings of our joy as Christians are infinitely deeper than the sources of our tears. *"Alleluia"* is our song.

Secondly, God has revealed Himself not only as Father, but also as the *Logos,* the Word. This revelation, too, must have deep significance for our Christian life. *Logos* means *word.* From all eternity, the Second Person of the Trinity infinitely "speaks" the greatness, the beauty, the goodness, the truth of the Father.

Hence St. Paul could say: Christ is the *"Amen"* to the Father. But He needs no "words" with which to speak. His entire infinite Personality is in Itself an infinitely eloquent *yes* to the Father as truth, as beauty, as goodness. We might say that from all eternity the Word is the "praise" of the Father. And since it was the *Logos,* the Word, who became man, and by baptism has made us His members and His brothers, does it not follow that our first and chiefest obligation as sons of God and brothers of Christ—in fact that our *total* obligation, which includes all else—is that we also "praise" the Father? That we say "yes" to Him by worship?

Thus baptism, by its very nature, points to worship. By this sacrament we have become able to share in the Second Person's infinite praise of the Father, particularly by means of the holy Sacrifice of the Mass. St. Thomas, accordingly, tells us that the character of baptism means deputation to cult. In the Mass, moreover, each major part is fittingly introduced by a baptismal prayer: Psalm 42 at the foot of the altar is a baptismal psalm. The *Credo,* introducing the Mass of the Faithful, is a great baptismal prayer. And so too is the Our Father, introducing the holy Communion service. As baptized, therefore, we should keenly appreciate this great privilege that is ours: to be united with Christ in infinite worship of the Father. "It is desirable, venerable brethren, that all the faithful shall be aware that to participate in the Eucharistic Sacrifice is their chief duty and supreme dignity" (Pope Pius XII in *Mediator Dei,* n. 80).

And finally, the Third Person has been revealed to us as Love. And St. Paul tells us that we are His temples by baptism. Now a temple has only one purpose: that of worship. Our whole life as baptized Christians, therefore, should be worship: a love-inspired and love-directed worship.

Carlyle in *Sartor Resartus* says, "The man who does not wonder, who does not habitually wonder, is like a pair of spectacles behind which there are no eyes." Our lives would be transformed if we had a due degree of wonder at the great and marvelous gifts that were granted to us in our baptism. And this good news could not fail to stimulate us to good action. *Noblesse oblige.*

V. UNTO FULL STATURE

We are probably familiar with baptism as the sacrament of *initiation*. Such of course it is. But it is only the first step of the complete initiation into Christ. According to the most ancient and unanimous Christian tradition, there are three sacraments of initiation: baptism, confirmation, and the Eucharist. (And it is no accident that these three are enumerated first and in that order in our listing of the seven sacraments.) Only with these three does a person experience the full Christian life; only through them can he grow unto full stature. That these three belong together is brought out already by the fact that, for centuries, they were conferred together in immediate succession.

In other words, in order to understand baptism more adequately, we cannot view it in isolation, but must consider it in relation to confirmation and the Eucharist. These three are a sort of sacramental trinity, by which the life of the Trinity, of the triune God, comes to fruition in us.

Let us recall that Christianity is not so much a doctrine, a philosophy, or even a way of life. It is rather a *fact* in which we must take part. That fact is Christ the Redeemer, living and active among us in His redemptive acts. "My delights were to be with the children of men."[1] Christianity is an historical religion, yes; but it is a contemporary, a present divine fact too— and *for us* that is even more relevant. The Church is not merely a society historically founded by the God-man, in which the business of salvation is infallibly dispensed to successive generations of men. Christ becomes incarnate, is incarnate, in each generation, in our generation—as Cardinal Suhard stressed in his magnificent pastoral, *Growth or Decline*.[2] Christ the *Redeemer* is speaking when He says: "I am with you all days, even unto

Liturgical Week 1948, Boston, Mass.
[1] Prov. 8:31.
[2] (South Bend, Ind.: Fides Press, 1948).

the consumation of the world."[3] He is *active* in our midst *as* Redeemer: His redemptive work is re-enacted, is realized in the liturgy, in the sacraments above all. As St. Leo the Great phrased it in a monumental sentence: "What was visible in the life of Christ has passed over into the sacraments."[4] The sacraments, the liturgy, is the continuation of the sublime mystery of the Son's epiphany among men.

It is Christ the High Priest who is the true minister, the principal agent, in all the sacraments. The human priest acts in the person of Christ (as St. Thomas tells us in so many words). In the Eucharist Christ is present substantially. But in the other sacraments, too, Christ is present.[5] In them the glorified Christ acts in and through His lawfully constituted ministers. The other sacraments can then be considered as so many activities by which Christ prepares us for fullest incorporation and union with Him in the Eucharist. The redeeming act, realized perfectly and to the full in the Eucharist, is *extended* through and by means of the other sacraments. In fact, St. Thomas does not hesitate to state that the other sacraments partake somehow even of the sacrificial character of the Eucharist.[6]

Applying this to the discussion of the three sacraments of initiation, I intend to follow the lead which St. Cyril of Jerusalem has given us in his *Catecheses*, composed about the year 350. (His witness enjoys a special authority: for he was declared a Doctor of the Church on the basis of his teaching concerning baptism, confirmation, and the Eucharist.)[7]

According to St. Cyril, baptism is not merely the remission of sin, or further, the grace of adoption. He insists, with all the eloquence at his command, that it is *first of all* a sharing, through the sacramental sign, in the passion and resurrection

---

[3] Matt. 28:20.

[4] *Quod itaque Redemptoris nostri conspicuum fuit, in sacramenta transivit*, Serm. 74, 2, For the Ascension (P.L. LIV, 398).

[5] Cf. encyclical, *Mediator Dei*, especially nos. 20, 165.

[6] *Summa Theologica*, III, q. 73, a. 4, ad 2.

[7] Recently some scholars have inclined to the view that St. Cyril is not the author of the five final "mystagogical catecheses" which here chiefly come into question, but that these derive from his successor, John. Even if this were proved, their doctrinal importance remains unimpaired.

of Christ. He insists that St. Paul's famous description of baptism in Romans, chapter 6, must be taken literally: we are baptized, i.e., dipped, plunged into, Christ's death and rising. (Remission of sin, receiving of life, is the *result*, not the primary thing that happens in baptism.)

Our baptism, then, is our entry, our introit, into Christ's glorious Passion and death in a most real sense: not as a result of our striving, not depending on human effort and will, but as a gratuitous gift of God. Our sharing in the passion and resurrection of Christ through baptism points to our sharing in Christ's passion and resurrection which is the Mass. Baptism derives its efficacy from the Cross: and so the baptized Christian must of necessity tend toward the Cross, the Mass. We must instinctively strive for the Mass, exercise *our new life* and character in the Mass. In baptism Christians have become sharers in the priesthood of Christ. Exercising that priesthood, offering the Holy Sacrifice of the Mass in the manner possible to them (i.e., through and with the ordained priest) is, as the Council of Trent says, the greatest act the baptized laity can perform. Or, as St. Thomas tells us succinctly, baptism is a deputation to cult.

Moreover, just as by nature we instinctively eat and drink, so instinctively, by the supernatural instinct which is the Holy Spirit operative within us, we must desire the *lac et mel*, the food of the Eucharist. As an infant instinctively searches for its mother's breast, so the baptized must yearn to be filled at the breasts of his spiritual Mother's consolation: *quasimodo geniti infantes*. He must *instinctively* yearn: forced feeding is a sign of ill health. When therefore reception of Holy Communion had to be imposed by law in the thirteenth century (called by some "the greatest"!) it was a sign that the spiritual disease infecting Christendom was already well advanced. Receiving Holy Communion should not be the result of legal pressure: it should be an internal urge! Here especially is it true that *caritas Christi urget nos*, "the charity of Christ impels us."

This relation of baptism to the Eucharist is clearly manifest in our present Mass rite. The Mass as a whole is introduced by the *Asperges*, the great sacramental of baptism. Then the Creed, which is the solemn renewal of our baptismal vows, leads us into the Mass of the Faithful. And the great baptismal prayer, the Our Father, invites us to approach the holy table.

Of confirmation, St. Cyril says: "Having been baptized into Christ, and put on Christ, you have been made conformable to the Son of God. . . . Being therefore made partakers of Christ, you are properly called 'Christs,' and of you God said: 'Touch not my Christs, or anointed.' Now you were made Christs by receiving the seal of the Holy Ghost; and all things were in an image (or sign: sacrament) wrought in you, because you are the images of Christ."[8] Then he describes how Christ was anointed by the Holy Ghost at the Jordan, that He might now begin His public ministry; and how what happened to Christ happens also to us by the anointing with holy chrism which we call confirmation. "Thus truly," he concludes, "we have been made partakers and fellows of Christ."

The sharing in the priestly power, initially conferred by baptism, is complemented therefore by the sharing in priestly power conferred in confirmation. In the latter case, however, it is more specifically the priestly power to be exercised in *our public ministry,* i.e., in our relations with our fellow men, in the service of holy Church. And as Christ's public ministry led up to and culminated in His glorious sacrificial death, so our life as confirmed, too, finds its magnet, or rather, its source and fulfillment in the Holy Sacrifice. As Christ was impelled by the Holy Ghost to enter into His glorious death, so we likewise are driven by the Holy Spirit of love to surrender ourselves with Christ in holy Mass. And this surrender, and it alone, can give true value and efficacy to our life of apostolate or "ministry."

About the Holy Eucharist, as treated by St. Cyril, it is enough to state that it means the ultimate and most complete union with Christ. By it, he says, we become *concorporei et consanguinei,* "of the same flesh and blood." The Eucharist, in a word, is at the same time the *source* and the *goal* of baptism and confirmation.

Baptism, confirmation, and the Eucharist therefore are the sacramental foundations of full Christian life and living. I would like to draw an important conclusion, namely, that the

[8] Third Mystagogical Catechesis.

Christian virtues, by which our Christian life is exercised, can be understood and practiced rightly only in terms of these sacraments: they have their source in and become operative chiefly through them. The life of virtue (Christian morals) is not a separate compartment of Christian living: it makes sense only as the overflow of the sacraments; it is rooted radically in the sacraments.

I think a good illustration of that fact can be found in the case of the greatest of the virtues, the theological virtues of faith, hope, and charity. Strictly speaking, all three are infused, or intensified, by each of the sacraments. And yet there is also a special correlation between this trinity of basic sacraments and this trinity of basic virtues. Baptism is in a very real sense the sacrament of faith, confirmation the sacrament of hope, and the Holy Eucharist the sacrament of charity.

Baptism and faith. These are associated constantly in Scripture: e.g., "He who believes and is baptized shall be saved."[9] In the rite of baptism, too, the association is striking: "What dost thou seek of the Church of God?" "Faith." "What doth faith bring thee to?" "Life everlasting." It would almost seem as if faith and not baptism itself were the important thing at stake in this rite. And the positive baptismal vows (not the negative renunciations) are phrased in terms of faith: "Do you *believe* in God the Father, etc." Hence, also, by common usage the baptized are simply called "the faithful." And St. Thomas casually remarks: "Baptism is called the sacrament of faith, which is the foundation of the spiritual life."[10]

Confirmation in its turn corresponds more to the virtue of hope. As at Pentecost, the Holy Spirit in confirmation is sent upon the faithful in His role as Paraclete, as the Comforter, the Strengthener. They are anointed *ad robur*: that they may be strong in doing Christian battle; that they may have *courage* in facing the superhuman tasks of the apostolate that lie ahead. Especially in our day, fear gnaws at the hearts and robs them of strength, undermines their courage to work. The great temptation of modern times is despair. It is the terrible reaction to the

9 Mark 16:16.
10 *Summa Theologica,* III, q. 73, a. 3, ad 3.

false optimism, the human self-reliance which characterized Western civilization from the age of humanism, through the Renaissance, the age of enlightenment, and the scientific age. Courage and hope, *hope in God*, is what we desperately need to live human, Christian lives. That is perhaps one reason why Peguy, the prophet and singer of hope, finds such an eager audience today. Only the divine Comforter, strengthening us in His sacrament, can be the sure foundation of hope. It is not a mere accident of theological history that the sacrament of confirmation, and devotion to the Holy Spirit, are being stressed today more than ever before. Only in the strength of divine hope can the confirmed lay apostle dare to work in and for a de-Christianized world, as the apostles dared, after Pentecost, to brave a pagan and unchristianized empire. Only as a confirmed Christian can he rationally avoid being overwhelmed by the black night of despair. "Now may the God of hope fill you with all joy and peace . . . that you may abound in hope and in the power of the Holy Spirit."[11]

> Thou of Comforters the best,
> Thou the soul's most welcome guest,
> Sweet refreshment here below.
>
> In our labor, rest most sweet,
> Grateful coolness in the heat,
> Solace in the midst of woe.[12]

Now there remain these three: faith, hope, and charity; but the greatest of these is charity. Now there are these three: baptism, confirmation, and the Holy Eucharist; but the greatest of these is the Eucharist.

That the *Eucharist* is above all and before all else the sacrament of *charity* needs no elaborate proof. Scripture and tradition, our own Christian conscience, bear joyful and unanimous witness. As Sacrifice, it is the re-enactment of Christ's *loving* surrender of Himself for us, even unto death. As Banquet it is a communion, a love-meal that unites the whole family of God to one another by uniting them to Christ. It was at the *Last*

---

[11] Rom. 15:13.
[12] Pentecost Sequence.

Supper that Christ told us about the vine and branches, and delivered His burning discourse on fraternal charity. And St. Paul, in I Corinthians, written to heal a schism, to overcome fraternal *un*charity, observes the same sequence: in chapter 11 he reports the institution of the Eucharist, in chapter 12 he gives us his famous description of the Mystical Body, and in chapter 13 he sings his canticle of praise of fraternal charity. "We, though many, are *one body*, all of us who partake of the one bread," he declares.[13] *Sacramentum unitatis, vinculum caritatis*, "the sacrament of unity, the bond of charity," St. Augustine calls the Eucharist. And St. Thomas Aquinas, in his turn, emphasizes nothing so much in his articles on the Eucharist as that "the fruit of this sacrament is the unity of the mystical body."[14] Holy Communion is the sacrament that builds up the communion of saints. Leo XIII rightly therefore reminds us that the frequent meeting at the common Eucharistic meal was the reason why the early Christians loved one another as they did. They were of one mind and one heart *because* they persevered in common prayer and the Breaking of Bread. Nor is it mere chance, and nothing more, that in our own day Pius X's decrees on frequent Communion preceded in point of time our reawakening to the doctrine of the Mystical Body, the doctrine of our common life and love and brotherhood. Man needed a special commandment ordering him to love his fellow man; and Christ gave man a special sacrament enabling him to carry out this command: the sacrament of the Eucharist.

Baptism, confirmation, and the Eucharist: faith, hope, and charity. And as baptism and confirmation lead up to and are perfected in the Eucharist so also the faith of baptism and the hope of confirmation are stirred up, renewed, and perfected in the charity of the Eucharist.

The faith of the baptized nowhere becomes more operative than in Holy Mass. The entire instruction part of the Mass (the so-called Mass of the Catechumens) has the one purpose of deepening the faith of the participants (*fides ex auditu*— "faith is from hearing"). And the Sacrifice proper, the *Mys-*

[13] I Cor. 10:17.
[14] *Summa Theologica*, III, q. 73, a. 3.

terium fidei, the Mass of the *Faithful,* is the great public act of faith of the entire Church in her crucified and risen Savior.

Similarly, the hope of the confirmed finds its public and solemn expression above all in the celebration of the Eucharist. There the zeal of the lay apostle finds its final consecration; there his hopeful activity in the cause of God becomes united to the redeeming activity of Christ Himself, to the *actio;* the action of the Mass. There he learns to obey the injunction of Christ: not only to give up what is hindering his advance, but the decisive "Come, *follow Me.*" Follow Me—no questions asked about why and whereunto, no if's and but's. It is the courageous plunge into the unknown, the complete surrender to God's holy will, which only hope, when rooted in charity, when strengthened by the Sacrifice and Sacrament of Charity, dares venture.

I have attempted to show, thus briefly, how the three sacraments of initiation, the sacraments that bring us the fullness of Christ-life, are also the sources of Christian *living* by means of the three theological virtues. Only because we *have* the Christ-life can we perform Christlike actions. And *because* we have the life, we *must* act in a Christlike manner. The gift becomes an obligation. This is true not only in regard to the theological virtues, but also in regard to the moral virtues. It all seems too obvious. For it is nothing else than the application of the universally valid principle, *agere sequitur esse,* "action follows being." A thing must act according to its being. It *is* all so obvious when expressed thus in principle. And yet how we have managed to obscure it in practice to our very, very great spiritual loss! We have made of Christianity a system of moralizing—do this and don't do that, almost as if we were still in the Old Testament. Christian life becomes a matter of laboriously striving to imitate the example of Christ, a painful and discouragingly slow process, in which we are helped by the grace of God, and in which we persevere because we want to get to heaven (or perhaps, really, only to avoid hell). The emphasis is almost solely on *our* effort.

What is worst of all, underlying this outlook and basically vitiating our effort, is a sort of hidden Pelagianism: the unconscious assumption that we ourselves can and must work out our own salvation. Cardinal Villeneuve of Quebec spoke once of the many-headed hydra of Pelagianism which crops up constantly through the ages. It threatens especially in our moralistic emphases. It was present and widespread at the time of the Reformation.[15] People had to a large extent lost contact with the sacraments: they failed to appreciate that it is through the sacraments that Christ redeems us; moral effort became separated from its sacramental sources, which alone make it possible and fruitful. Christian action had become disjointed from Christian being. The moral emphasis superseded the sacramental, or ontological. And the result was less morality; and what there was of it was a dreary enough process. People were worlds apart from Christianity as a "glad tidings," from the "making melody in your hearts" to which St. Paul exhorts us. But are we not, too?

Agere sequitur esse. Action *follows* being. Christian living is possible only because of God's life in us.

Christ Himself indicated the right order of things: "Go, therefore, and make disciples of all nations, *baptizing* them in the name of the Father, and of the Son, and of the Holy Spirit, teaching them *to observe* all things whatsoever I have commanded you."[16] In virtue of the sacraments Christ lives and Christ operates in us. His image has been impressed on us by baptism and confirmation, is constantly being renewed and deepened in us by Holy Communion. Now we *can* and must show forth that image to angels and to men in our actions. St. Paul, who exults in his calling, in his election, does not cease telling us: "You *have* put on Christ" (in the sacraments); and in the same breath, as it were, he continues, "Therefore, put ye on Christ" (in your actions). It is not a question of doing less, of less effort on our part in virtuous acts; God forbid. It is a question of doing *more* and doing it differently, in a new vision of faith: of doing it confidently and joyfully, because we know that in Him, in Christ, we can do all things.

Christianity is a glad tidings, not a hard bargain which God

[15] See the remarkable study by Joseph Lortz, *Die Reformation in Deutschland*, 2 vols. (2nd ed.; Freiburg im Breisgau: Herder, 1941).
[16] Matt. 28:19–20.

drives with man. We are not mere creatures, doing our best, and hoping for a future union with God as a reward.

This relationship of morals and sacraments is beautifully illustrated in some of the early sacramental texts. Thus St. Hippolytus in his *Apostolic Tradition* (a. 213), after describing the Paschal Mass, adds: "And when these things (i.e., the Communion rites) have been accomplished, let each one hasten to do good works, to please God and to live aright, devoting himself to the Church, practicing the things he has learned, advancing in the service of God" (n. 23). And St. Justin Martyr, a full generation earlier, having described the sacraments of initiation, states: "And we afterwards continually remind one another of these things. And the wealthy among us help the needy; and we always keep together; and for all things wherewith we are supplied, we bless the Maker of all through His Son Jesus Christ."[17]

If the first centuries of the Church were a springtime of Christian living, the reason is to be sought in a vivid realization of the height of divine life and dignity to which God's love had raised them by the sacraments.[18] St. Leo's "O Christian, remember thy dignity" could be multiplied an indefinite number of times. But God's arm is not shortened. The fountains of grace spring up as fresh and abundantly now as in those times. Or rather, since Pius X's decree of frequent and daily Communion, those fountains are more available to us than they were to the first generation's Christians. The fruit of moral and holy lives should not be lacking.

Holy Mother Church urges us, therefore, in a beautiful Secret prayer that she uses twice, on the fourth Sunday after Easter and the Eighteenth after Pentecost: "O God, who through our sharing in this revered Sacrifice, dost make us partakers of the one supreme Godhead: grant we beseech Thee, that having come to an understanding of (this) Thy truth, we may realize it (i.e., carry it into practice) by worthy lives.

[17] *First Apology*, 67.
[18] A realization so vivid that for several centuries the discipline of only one penance in a lifetime generally obtained. Our Christian ancestors had a sense of height, and consequently also of depth: a horror for sin.

Through Christ our Lord." And the *Ite, missa est* at the end of
Mass is the solemn echo by the Church of Christ's solemn com-
mand: Why do you stand all the day idle? *Ite in vineam meam!*
Go you also into My vineyard!

From all the above, it should be evident that the life of virtue
is not a separate department of Christian life, but is based on,
and should be the overflow of, the three sacraments of initiation.
That the mystical has the same basis and is a similar overflow
may need even more emphasis. In the eyes of most, the mystical
life is something quite remote, esoteric, and very rare. There
seems to be such a separation between it and the ordinary life
of the sacraments, or the normal Christian living, that few dare
to aspire to it. In fact, most look upon it almost with suspicion.
And that means, to put it boldly, that we have been deprived
of our great and rightful heritage.

In our own day, owing largely to a renewed appreciation of
the role of the sacraments in Christian perfection, there is also
a growing conviction that the mystical life is an organic flowering and development of the divine life given us in the sacraments; that it is not a *new* world, but the divine operation of
the sacraments in its highest form.[19]

The historical description of the spiritual life in terms of the
purgative, illuminative, and unitive way may be said to correspond to the sacraments of baptism, confirmation, and the
Eucharist. Baptism is a permanent sacrament, the permanent
basis of the purgative life. (In comparison to confirmation, baptism does stress more the aspect of renunciation, detachment.)
Confirmation in turn activates the illuminative way: it is the
life-long divine anointing for positive progress in the life of virtue, for correspondence to the gifts of the Spirit. In the Eucharist, finally, we have the source of the unitive way. In it we
are granted the highest objective, sacramental, union with the

---

19 Cf. Garrigou-Lagrange, *Christian Perfection and Contemplation*
(which interprets the doctrine of St. Thomas); Anselm Stolz, *Doctrine of Christian Perfection* (which presents the same thesis on the
basis of the Fathers). See also Abbot Butler's *Western Mysticism* and
Stolz's article "Mysticism as Normal Flowering of the Sacramental
Life," *Orate Fratres*, XVII, 393–97, 447–55.

God-man, a union of love which then becomes a subjective experience in contemplation.[20]

The same conclusion, of relationship between these three sacraments and the "stages" of the spiritual life, is brought out luminously in a traditional description of these sacraments, found especially in the Eastern Fathers and in our liturgy. Presupposing St. John's preferred figure of Spouse and Bride, the Eucharist as "Covenant" is the nuptial feast, the love feast of Christ and His Bride. Baptism and confirmation, in turn, are the preparation of the Bride for this nuptial celebration. Baptism, in this context, corresponds to the ancient custom of the ceremonial bath, a holy cleansing, of the bride. St. Paul had this in mind when he wrote: "Husbands, love your wives, just as Christ also loved the Church, and delivered himself up for her, that he might sanctify her, *cleansing her in the bath of water* . . . that he might present to himself the Church . . . not having spot or wrinkle . . . without blemish."[21] It is the underlying thought also of the famous *Benedictus* antiphon for the feast of Epiphany: "Today the Church has been joined to her celestial Bridegroom . . . for in the Jordan, Christ washed away her faults" (Baptism, accordingly, is the "purgation" of the Bride, or the people of God). After the ceremonial washing and cleansing, the bride was then ceremoniously anointed with precious ointments—as the Church was anointed by the Spirit at Pentecost, as the faithful are anointed in the sacrament of confirmation (cf. confirmation as "illumination"). Thus prepared, the bride was led to the bridegroom; thus prepared, by baptism and confirmation, the Bride of Christ, the Church, advances to the nuptial feast of Eucharistic union—the nuptials which rejoice the Bride in contemplative union.[22]

In fine, baptism, confirmation, and the Eucharist contain essentially the whole story of man's love-union with Christ: they

[20] A classical description of the three sacraments of initiation and their flowering in the mystical life is that of Nicolas Cabasilas (d. 1371), *De vita in Christo* (P.G. CL, 493–726).
[21] Eph. 5:25 ff.
[22] Cf. Odo Casel, "Die Taufe als Brautbad der Kirche," *Jahrbuch fuer Liturgiewissenschaft*, V, 144–47.

are the foundation on which all else is built—the life of virtue, the life also of mystical union. "I exhort you, therefore, to walk in a manner worthy of the calling with which you were called . . . until we all attain . . . to perfect manhood, to the mature measure of the fullness of Christ."[23]

23 Eph. 4:1, 13.

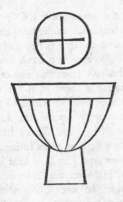

PART THREE

I. WITH CHRIST IN THE MASS

Perhaps it will not be superfluous to begin this chapter by re-calling that the holy Eucharist (understood in its full meaning, as Sacrifice as well as Food) is a *sacrament*. Now sacraments are external signs by which Christ the God-man carries out and applies His work of redemption through the centuries. Christ's promise, "I shall be with you all days even to the consummation of the world" (Matt. 28:20), refers not merely to His guidance of the Church in doctrine and morals. He came to give *life*, and to give it more abundantly. He is with us, He is operative in our midst, above all in the sacraments, whereby He gives us the more abundant life.

This is simply another manner of saying that Christ is the chief minister of all the sacraments. Christ in His passion and resurrection (which summarize His redemptive work) reaches out into time, embraces man, consecrates man, lifts man up to identify him more and more with Himself. "The Word became man, that man might become God," St. Leo the Great loved to remind us. Christ is the *Way*: not merely God's way to us, but our way to God. Through the sacraments we can enter upon and walk that way.

Liturgical Week 1947, Portland, Ore.

In other words: although the sacraments are *"propter homines,"* for the benefit of man inasmuch as they are channels of grace or the way of God's grace to us, that is not their ultimate and most important purpose. (Perhaps we have been accustomed to regard them too exclusively from this aspect: we like to apply the pragmatic test: what is there in it for me, or at best, for us?) Not man is the real, final *terminus* of the sacraments, but God. We do not merely *receive* the sacraments. But by every sacrament we are lifted up, Christ lifts us up, unto God. By every sacrament we become more intimately identified with Christ our High Priest and Head, so that being one with Him we may join Him in His foremost and most essential task: to give glory to the Father. In fine: every sacrament is in its ultimate and deepest purpose *worship*.

The Eucharist of course is the center and climax of the sacraments. It is Christ's great sacrifice re-enacted. Christ commanded: "Do this in memory of Me." And the Church carries out that command, does it in holy Mass. That the Eucharist is the sacrifice of Christ, which the Church, in Christ's name and in His person, offers to God the Father, belongs to the ABC's of our religion. It has been expressly defined by the Council of Trent. It is the cornerstone of our Christian life and worship.

Our question in this chapter is: What part precisely have the people of God, the congregation, the laity, in this sacrifice?

Before answering, I would like to make clear what I consider a basic distinction. In every sacrifice there must be two things: (1) the act of offering (which presupposes an offerer), and (2) the thing offered (the victim).

(1) As to the *offering* in the Eucharist. Christ on Calvary offered the all-perfect sacrifice of His Body and Blood for us, *pro nobis.* "For us" means, however, not only for our benefit, but also *in our stead.* That is precisely why He became man, that, as Head of the sinful human race, as *representing* us, He might offer this sacrifice of reconciliation and of new life in the sacrifice of Calvary He offered in our stead. That is to say, all of us were implicitly offering through Him. And Calvary is re-enacted in holy Mass as sacrifice primarily that what was done by sinful mankind *implicitly* on Calvary, might now be done by them explicitly, consciously. On Calvary, by the very

nature of Christ's sacrifice, we were implicitly co-offerers with Christ. In holy Mass, we are privileged to co-offer the sacrifice with Him explicitly, as responsible human agents, with understanding and grateful hearts. (I shall come back to this point later.)

(2) As to the *Victim offered*. There is only one Victim that is capable of reconciling man and God, and that is Christ: the Lamb of God who taketh away the sins of the world. The Blood of Christ alone is able to wash away our sins; and its value is superabundant. "Behold the wood of the Cross, on which hung the Salvation of the world. Come, let us adore." There is only one Mediator of the New Testament, only one Victim, unique and absolute, and that is the Man-God Jesus Christ.

In holy Mass, therefore, the re-enactment of Calvary, we can and must be co-offerers with Christ; but we cannot be co-victims in the same sense. We come to Mass in order humbly and gratefully to join Christ in offering *His* sacrificial Body and Blood. Holy Mass is the rite by which Christ is offered to the Father. When we join in that offering, we should of course strive to unite our minds and wills *with the Victim*. Like the drop of water mingled with the precious wine, we as it were "hide behind" the all-perfect Victim, we ask to be accepted by the Father in union with Christ our sacrificial Gift. And the fruit we personally derive from the sacrifice will be in exact proportion to the victimhood of our hearts. But we can add nothing to that perfect and all-holy oblation. In more precise terms: we are true, actual co-offerers with Christ; but we can be co-victims with Him only in what we might call a moral sense. Or to put it in another way: holy Mass is a golden opportunity for us to be co-victims with Christ, an opportunity that dare not be neglected; but holy Mass *in itself* is solely and alone the offering up of the unique and infinitely holy Victim which is Jesus Christ. We come to Mass to offer Christ to the Father.

Now to come back to the main point of this chapter. How, and by what right, can and should the laity actively co-offer the Holy Eucharist with the priest, with the Church, with Christ? That they can and should do so needs little proof. We have already seen that it is demanded by the very nature of Christ's

Sacrifice. For He offered *in our stead:* which means that we must now consciously join Him in that act of offering.

The matter is made clear to us beyond the possibility of doubt by the prayers of holy Mass itself. Again and again the priest uses the word *"offerimus,"* "we offer." No other thought, in fact, is so often repeated or given such prominence in the ordinary of the Mass. Nor can the *offerimus* be explained away as a mere majestic plural, or as a relic of the time when bishop and priests concelebrated (so it would refer only to those in holy orders). Because at least twice, in the canon itself, it is expressly stated that the *people* themselves also offer. In the first Memento prayer, the celebrant prays: "Be mindful, O Lord, . . . of all here present, . . . for whom we offer, or *who themselves offer up to Thee this Sacrifice of Praise."*[1] And the prayer immediately following the consecration states: "Wherefore we Thy servants, and *likewise Thy holy people,* . . . offer unto Thy most excellent majesty . . . a pure Victim. . . ." (Note also that it is the divine Victim they are said to offer: not just themselves.) The doctrinal weight of these two texts can hardly be exaggerated. For the official canon of the Church's prayer is an infallible expression of the Church's faith (*"lex orandi—lex credendi"*).

As one instance of how traditional this manner of speaking is, I will quote from the Doctor of the Eucharist, St. John Chrysostom—a doctor, incidentally, who stands for down-to-earth, literal language and interpretation as against the Alexandrian metaphorical trend. In his eighteenth homily on Second Corinthians he writes:

[1] It is of considerable interest to note that originally only the second clause, "who themselves offer up to Thee this sacrifice of praise— *qui tibi offerunt hoc sacrificium laudis,"* was contained in this prayer. But already in Carolingian times, when active participation of the laity had largely lapsed, some clerical minds felt disturbed by such a clear statement of the laity's role in the sacrifice, and the clause *"pro quibus tibi offerimus*—for whom we offer" was added. (In some cases, indeed, the "offending" clause was entirely omitted.) This addition very likely goes back to Alcuin (d. 804), certainly to his circle.—Cf. J. A. Jungmann, S.J., "Die Abwehr des germanischen Arianismus und der Umbruch der religioesen Kultur in fruehen Mittelalter," *Zeitschrift fuer kath. Theologie,* LXIX, 1 (1947), 95.

"It is true that at the heart of these tremendous mysteries (of the Eucharist) the priest prays on behalf of the people—but the people also pray on behalf of him: that and nothing else is the meaning of the response 'And with your spirit.' Even the Eucharist [the prayer of consecration] is a common prayer; the priest does not give thanks alone but all the people with him. I admit that it is the priest who takes the leading part, but please notice that he does not begin the eucharistic prayer until you have given him leave by declaring that to do so is a worthy and righteous act [a reference to the *'Dignum et justum est'* response]. You need have no surprise that the people join in with the priest when his own voice is joined with those of the cherubim and all the heavenly host in the holy song of the angels [the *Sanctus*]. I have said all this, my brethren, in order that each one of you, even he who feels himself the lowliest of all, may be attentive at these holy Mysteries, that we may realize that we are all one Body. . . . So do not leave everything to the clergy but interest yourselves in all that is the concern of the whole Church, as befits those who form but one Body."[2]

And even more clearly, bringing all tradition to a head, as it were, Pope Pius XI in his encyclical on the reparation due to the Sacred Heart (*"Miserentissimus Redemptor,"* May 8, 1928) declares:

"The Apostle admonished us that . . . having become partakers in His holy and eternal priesthood, we should offer up 'gifts and sacrifices for sins' (Heb. 5:1). For not only are they partakers in the mystery of this priesthood and in the duty of offering sacrifices and satisfaction to God, who have been appointed by Jesus Christ the High Priest as the ministers of such sacrifices, to offer God 'a clean oblation in every place from the rising of the sun even to the going down' (Mal. 1:10), but also those Christians called, and rightly so, by the Prince of the Apostles, 'a chosen generation, a kingly priesthood' (1 Pet. 2:9), who are to offer 'sacrifices for sin' (Heb. 5:1) not only for themselves but for all mankind, and this in much the

[2] Migne *P.G.* 61, 527. The translation is quoted from Donald Attwater's *St. John Chrysostom* (Milwaukee: The Bruce Publishing Co., 1939), pp. 193 ff.

same way as every priest (*haud aliter propemodum quam sacerdos omnis*) and 'high priest taken from among men is ordained for man in the things that appertain to God'" (Heb. 5:1). This passage moreover occurs in a second nocturn lesson of the fourth day in the Sacred Heart octave, and thus gets additional force from its liturgical usage.

Rightly, therefore, from most ancient times, the celebrant has always invited the congregation: "*Gratias agamus Domino Deo nostro*": let us together offer this rite of thanksgiving, this Eucharist. And when the great prayer-act of thanksgiving has been completed, all the people should give witness to their participation by answering "*Amen*"—that is to say: "You have spoken and acted for us too." (Cf. the importance attached to this "Amen" by St. Justin Martyr in his *First Apology*, ch. 65.)

A recent author, considered by many as an outstanding modern theologian of the Mystical Body, the Jesuit Fr. Sebastian Tromp of Rome, does not hesitate to say: "That both the Church herself, as well as the faithful, the members of the Church, actually offer in the Mass, must absolutely be held, and cannot be denied without grave rashness."[3]

Active participation of the laity in offering the holy Sacrifice is not therefore just a concession, or a means devised to keep the congregation attentive and perhaps more interested. It is demanded by the very nature of the Mass; it is demanded by the very dignity of Christians as members of Christ.

The *theological basis* for such co-offering is the fact that all baptized by virtue of their baptism have become members of Christ the High Priest and consequently share in His priesthood. This is ordinarily called the doctrine of the general priesthood, or perhaps less happily, the doctrine of the lay priesthood. We all know St. Peter's famous words concerning it: "You are a chosen generation, a kingly priesthood, a holy nation" (1 Pet. 2:9; cf. also 2:5). St. John too refers to it no less than three times in the Apocalypse (1:4-6; 5:9-10; 20:6). Of these, the first is perhaps the most striking: "Grace be unto you and peace . . . from Jesus Christ . . . who hath loved us . . . and made us a kingdom, and priests to God and His Father." This

---

[3] "Quo sensu in Sacrificio Missae offerat Ecclesia, offerant fideles," *Periodica de re morali, canonica, liturgica,* XXX (1941) 266.

passage was, by the way, incorporated into the liturgy of the Feast of the Most Precious Blood and of Christ the King, during the pontificate of Pius XI, the pope of Catholic Action, thus emphasizing its actual, present relevance.

The testimony of tradition about this doctrine, which still seems so "new" to many of us, has been gathered by several Catholic authors within the past decade. For our purposes it will suffice to cite, first of all, the eminent Doctor of the East, St. John Chrysostom: "You became king, priest and prophet in the bath of baptism."[4] Then St. Augustine, the greatest Doctor of the West: "In the same manner that we call all Christians, because of the mystic chrism, so we call all priests, because they are all members of the one Priest."[5] And finally St. Jerome, the jealous custodian of traditional teaching and prince of Scripture scholars: "The priesthood of the laity, i.e., baptism."[6]

The Scholastics, in their turn, contributed to the development of the doctrine in terms of the sacramental character. St. Thomas Aquinas with his characteristic precision states simply: "The sacramental character is nothing else than a certain participation in Christ's priesthood, deriving from Christ Himself."[7] I might add that insofar as Luther and the Reformers insisted on the general priesthood of the laity they insisted on good Catholic doctrine; their error lay in extending it unduly, in denying the specific powers of the priesthood of holy orders. But since they denied also the reality of the sacrifice, they emptied even the "lay priesthood" of its most precious content and meaning.

In reaction to the Protestant abuse of the term "priesthood of the laity," however, Catholic authors until very recent times not only stressed the special dignity of holy orders, but also tended to underestimate the general priesthood. Because St. Peter in his famous text exhorts the laity, "a holy priesthood, to offer *spiritual sacrifices*" (1 Pet. 2:5), they concluded that such a priesthood is only metaphorical, figurative: for it can offer, not a real sacrifice, but only figurative "sacrifices" of good works, prayer, a virtuous life, etc. (e.g., Pohle, the *Catholic Encyclo-*

[4] *In 2 Cor.*, hom. 3, 7; Migne *P.G.* 61, 417.
[5] *De Civitate Dei* 20, 10; Migne *P.L.* 41, 676.
[6] *Contra Luciferianos* 4; Migne *P.L.* 23, 158.
[7] *Summa Theologica*, III, q. 63, a. 3.

pedia under "Priesthood"). This objection has in fact become so widespread that it calls for a word of explanation.

The word "spiritual" (*pneumatikos*) as used by St. Peter is not the opposite of "real," but rather of "fleshly, material" (*sarkikos, physikos*). *Pneumatikos* is used twenty-seven times in the New Testament (not at all in the Old), twice in this chapter of St. Peter. All the other twenty-five passages in no way indicate the meaning "figurative" or "symbolical" or "unreal," but something in which the Holy Spirit, the *Pneuma*, has a part. Why then must we conclude that the texts of St. Peter consitute an exception?[8] Rather, the Eucharist (as the missal prayers themselves give testimony) is a "spiritual food" and it is the "*spiritualis hostia*." It is gratifying to note that the two most recent commentaries on St. Peter's First Epistle, one by a Catholic and the other by an Anglican, both conclude that his phrase "spiritual sacrifices" refers to the Eucharist at least inclusively if not primarily. The matter is placed beyond dispute for us by Pope Pius XI's encyclical quoted above: for he bases his statement about the laity's co-offering the eucharistic sacrifice directly on St. Peter's text.

The exact *manner* and *extent* of the laity's sharing in the priesthood and in the offering of the sacrifice is of course another matter, and one too vast and theologically involved to find a place in such a book as this. It may however not be out of place to suggest an approach to a solution. Perhaps it would clarify the question to say that the term "priesthood" is not identical with "holy orders," but is wider. There is only one Priest, Jesus Christ, and consequently one sole priesthood in the New Dispensation. His members share in that priesthood in progressive degrees: by the characters of baptism and confirmation for the laity—a partial sharing; by the character of holy orders, which confers the fullness. That is to say: although all three sacramental characters confer a true sharing in Christ's priesthood, baptism and confirmation do not mean a participation in the specific powers of holy orders.

Applying this to the Holy Eucharist, we may conclude that,

[8] Cf. E. Niebecker, *Das allgemeine Priestertum der Gläubigen* (Paderborn, 1936), pp. 90 ff.

as Christ on Calvary offered the sacrifice for our benefit, but also in our stead, so the ordained priest in holy orders offers, like Christ, in the name of and in the stead of the entire holy people, the congregation of the laity. But precisely because he ministers not only for them but in their stead, the laity can and should actively and intelligently participate in these holy Mysteries. To use the words of St. Robert Bellarmine, quoted by Fr. Tromp in the article already mentioned: "As Christ offers through the priest as through His inferior, so the faithful offer through the priest as through their superior" (p. 271). The laity truly offer the Sacrifice—they offer *with* the priest; but they cannot offer with him except by offering *through* him. And both together, priest and people, *in* the one High Priest, Jesus Christ, offer to the Father.

II. MARRIAGE OF CHRIST AND THE CHURCH

In the holy sacrifice of the Mass, at the most sacred moment of consecration, Mother Church puts words on the lips of the priest which at first hearing, seem rather mysterious: "This is the chalice of my blood, of the new and eternal testament (or covenant): the mystery of faith." And the scriptural accounts of the Last Supper have the identical idea, but clothed in slightly different words: e.g., "This cup is the new covenant in my blood" (Luke 22:20).

This reference to the new and eternal covenant is obviously intended to remind us of the old and temporary covenant which God established with his chosen people, the Jews. The type should help us understand the anti-type, or fulfillment. The word "covenant" means as much as agreement, treaty, compact, or contract. Now this contract or covenant of the old law is often represented in the inspired text as a marriage covenant, an espousal between God, Yahweh, and his people.

Liturgical Week 1946, Denver, Colo.

This interpretation of the old covenant as a spousal union is especially emphasized by the prophets—Isaias, Jeremaias, Ezechiel, Osee—who point out the infidelity of Israel as the bride of Yahweh. Perhaps most famous is the description in Ezechiel 16, where God, through the mouth of his prophet, condemns his bride for having been unfaithful. He reminds Israel how he rescued her from her filth and nakedness:

"Yea, I swore unto thee, and entered into a covenant with thee, and thou becamest mine. I clothed thee with richly woven work, and covered thee with silk. I decked thee also with ornaments . . . and put a beautiful crown upon thy head. . . . Thou wast meet for royal estate. And thy renown went forth among the nations for thy beauty; for it was perfect, through my splendor which I had put upon thee, saith the Lord God. But thou didst trust in thy beauty and play the harlot because of thy renown. . . . Thou wife that committest adultery, that takest strangers instead of thy husband. . . . I will satisfy my fury upon thee, I will bring thy way upon thine own head, saith the Lord God."[1]

The nature and terms of that covenant between God and Israel, his spouse, are made clear in Exodus 19. As we read the text, it is instructive to keep in mind, by way of contrast, the atmosphere of intimacy and love that characterized the Last Supper, the establishment of the new covenant:

"And Moses went up to God (on Mount Sinai). . . . And he (God) said to him: Go to the people, and let them be ready against the third day: for on that day the Lord will come down in the sight of all people upon Mount Sinai. And thou shalt appoint certain limits to the people round about and thou shalt say to them: Take heed you go not up into the Mount, and that ye touch not the borders thereof: every one that toucheth the Mount, dying he shall die. No hands shall touch him, but he shall be stoned to death, or shall be shot through with arrows: whether it be beast, or man, he shall not live. . . ."

And then, when the third day had come, God appeared amidst fire and smoke, and gave the Ten Commandments to Moses as the terms of his compact with Israel. The whole ac-

[1] Cf. also Os. 2:16–20; Is. 50:1; Jer. 2; 3; 31; 33.

count does not make for a very cheerful picture. One would hardly speak of it as an ideal spousal relationship. But God knew that Israel was a sinful people, stiff-necked, and prone to idolatry. And just as Israel, the spouse of God, proved unfaithful, and hence this nuptial union was a very imperfect thing, so also marriage itself in the Old Testament—which was sacred because through this espousal between God and his people it foreshadowed the nuptials of Christ and the Church—was a very imperfect marriage: its unity and indissolubility were both violated frequently, and God permitted it "because of the hardness of their hearts."

The old covenant was, of course, but a preparation for the new, the dawn before the brightness that was to come. And therefore also the basic relationship between Yahweh and his people was but a faint image of what was to be in the New Testament: Christ's union with his bride, the Church. Very often, in the Old Testament books, reference is made to this new spousal union, the perfect spousal union, which the Messias was to establish.[2] Paul summarizes it all in Gal. 4:21-31:

"Abraham had two sons, the one by a slave-girl and the other by a free woman (Agar—Sarah). This is said by way of allegory. For these are the two covenants: one indeed from Mount Sinai, bringing forth children unto bondage, which is Agar (the Church of the Old Testament); . . . But that Jerusalem which is above (the Church of the New Testament) is free, which is our mother. . . . Therefore, brethren, we are not children of a slave girl, but of the free woman."

The Old Testament union between God and Israel was a union with a slave-girl; the Church of the Old Testament was not so much a spouse as rather a handmaid, a servant—an unfaithful servant. The Church of the New Testament, however, is a free woman: and hence the union is a true union, a union, as it were, between equals. God became man, became our equal, that He might win for Himself his bride, and lift her up to His high estate.

As announced by the prophets, the true spousal relationship

[2] Cf. the entire *Canticle of Canticles;* Psalm 44, the psalm concerning the King and His bride; Os. 2:18; Is. 10:10; 62:4; etc.

between God and his people became a reality with the advent of the Savior. John the Baptist already had spoken of the Messias as the bridegroom, to whom alone his hearers must attach themselves: he himself was only the friend of the bridegroom, preparing the way for Him (John 3:28–29). Three of the evangelists, then, recount how Christ applied the title of bridegroom to Himself: "Jesus said to them: Can the children of the bridegroom mourn as long as the bridegroom is with them? But the days will come when the bridegroom shall be taken away from them, and then they shall fast" (Matt. 9:15. Cf. Mark 2:19 sq.; Luke 5:34 sq.). And finally, at the Last Supper, this new and eternal bridal covenant was instituted in the cup of His Blood, which was to be shed for them on Calvary.

In view of the Old Testament prophecies, in view especially of Christ's own words, it was to be expected that the disciples of Christ would likewise think and speak of the new covenant in terms of a spousal relationship. John in particular does so with predilection. He represents the union of Christ and the Church in two figures: that of the heavenly city, and that of a bridal union; and he prefers the latter. In Chapter 19 of the Apocalypse, for instance, he narrates his vision of the Church, the bride, participating in the glory and triumph of her spouse:

"Alleluia! For the Lord our God almighty now reigns! Let us be glad and rejoice, and give glory to him: for the marriage of the Lamb has come, and his spouse has prepared herself. And she has been permitted to clothe herself in fine linen, shining, bright. For the fine linen is the just deeds of the saints. And he said to me: Write: Blessed are they who are called to the marriage supper of the Lamb." (Cf. also Apoc. 21:2–9.)

St. Paul, too, uses the same figure. Thus, for example, he addresses the Church at Corinth: "For I betrothed you to one spouse, that I might present you a chaste virgin to Christ" (II Cor. 11:2). His most important text however is found in Chapter 5 of his letter to the Ephesians, the famous chapter in which he also treats so wonderfully of Christian marriage. This particular text is of special significance, for the Epistle to the Ephesians has the specific purpose of revealing to his hearers the great mystery of Christ's union with the Church:

"Yes, to me, the very least of all saints, there was given this grace, to announce among the Gentiles the good tidings of the unfathomable riches of Christ, and to enlighten all men as to what is the dispensation of the mystery which has been hidden from eternity in God (3:8–9) . . . and by reading you can perceive how well versed I am in the mystery of Christ, that mystery which in other ages was not known to the sons of men, as now it has been revealed to his holy apostles . . . in the Spirit: namely, that the Gentiles are joint heirs and fellow members of the same body (3:4–5)."

Chapter 5 itself is well known, of course, because it is used as the epistle of the nuptial Mass. I shall quote only the more relevant passages:

"Let wives be subject to their husbands as to the Lord (22); because a husband is head of the wife, just as Christ is head of the Church, being himself savior of the body (23). But just as the Church is subject to Christ, so also let wives be to their husbands in all things (24). Husbands, love your wives, just as Christ also loved the Church and delivered himself up for her (25), that he might sanctify her (26), that she might be holy and without blemish (27). Even thus ought husbands also to love their wives as their own bodies (28). He who loves his own wife, loves himself. For no one ever hated his own flesh; on the contrary he nourishes and cherishes it, as Christ also does the Church (29). 'For this reason a man shall leave his father and mother and shall cleave to his wife; and the two shall become one flesh' (31). This is a great mystery—I mean in reference to Christ and to the Church (32)."

It is evident that St. Paul here uses both concepts or metaphors—that of the Mystical Body, and that of spouse and bride —to teach us about the Church's (and our) life-union with Christ. In fact, it is interesting to note that in this same Epistle to the Ephesians, in which he speaks perhaps most explicitly of the Church as the Body of Christ, he also has his most explicit exposition of the Church as the bride of Christ (i.e., the above passage from Eph. 5). In this latter passage, indeed, the two figures are inextricably united and as it were merge into one another (cf. vv. 25, 28, 29, 31). This certainly suggests that the two concepts fundamentally say the same thing; that they supplement each other, are two aspects of the same truth. We may however go a step further, and ask: where did St. Paul get his metaphor of head and body?

It has always seemed to me that reference to Stoic concepts of society being a "body" current at his time is an insufficient answer. St. Paul was a Jew intimately acquainted with the Scriptures. He knew very well the Old Testament passages concerning Yahweh and the chosen people as spouse and bride, and the prophecies about the fulfillment of this type in Messianic times. Now from Eph. 5 we are led to suspect that the concept "spouse-bride" very naturally suggested the other concept of "head-body" to him: husband and wife become two in one flesh, and because the wife is subject to the husband, in that "two in one flesh" she constitutes the "body" and the husband the "head." At the very least one may be justified in concluding that the metaphor of the marriage bond between Christ and his Church was a source for his Mystical Body metaphor; and that, consequently, though he used the latter far more frequently, the former remains basic for a true understanding of his teaching concerning the life-relation between the Church and Christ.

While the spouse-bride figure therefore antedated that of the head-body (because used by Christ himself), and while it was the favorite comparison employed by St. John, St. Paul spoke so much of the Mystical Body that this figure can be said to outbalance that of the spouse-bride in New Testament usage. In tradition, however, the idea of Christ as the spouse and the Church as bride remained a favorite one.[3] One need only recall, e.g., the early representations of the Church in art, where she is pictured, as in the famous painting in the catacombs of St. Priscilla, in the form of a woman praying with outstretched arms (*Ecclesia Orans*). And the Fathers of the Church vied with each other in singing the praises of the spotless bride of Christ. In a paragraph that has become classical, St. Ambrose writes:

"So the holy Church, ignorant of wedlock, but fertile in bearing, is in chastity a virgin, and a mother in offspring. She, a virgin, bears us her children, not by a human father, but by the

---

[3] Especially in connection with the concept of the Church as mother. Cf. the excellent monograph by Dr. J. C. Plumpe: *Mater Ecclesia* (Catholic University Press, 1943).

Spirit. She bears us not with pain, but with the rejoicings of the angels. She, a virgin, feeds us, not with the milk of the body, but with that of the Apostle, wherewith he fed the tender age of the people who were still children (cf. I Cor. 3:2—the milk of doctrine). For what bride has more children than holy Church, who is a virgin in her sacraments and mother to her people, whose fertility even holy Scripture attests, saying, 'For many more are the children of the desolate than of her that hath a husband.' She has not a husband, but she has a bridegroom, inasmuch as, whether as the Church among nations, or as the soul in individuals, without any loss of modesty, she weds the Word of God as her eternal spouse, free from all injury, full of reason."[4]

St. Augustine too, who has special authority in this field since he is recognized as the "Doctor Ecclesiae," i.e., the Doctor who excels in treating about the Church, loves to develop the thought of the Church as the bride of Christ. In his explanation of the Psalms, in particular, he finds in this metaphor a rich source of spiritual applications.

It is above all in the Liturgy, however, that the relationship of Christ to his bride, the Church, is given full prominence. His great mysteries whereby he redeemed the world are celebrated in the liturgical year as so many manifestations of his nuptials with the Church. There is hardly a feast of the temporal cycle which does not underscore this truth. Examples could be cited in great number. I will limit myself to two, from feasts whose nuptial significance would scarcely be apparent to our rather prosaic Western way of thinking. The Benedictus antiphon for Lauds of Epiphany is perhaps the better known: "This day hath the Church been joined to her heavenly spouse, for Christ hath cleansed her crimes in the Jordan; with gifts the Magi hasten to the royal nuptials, and the wedding guests are gladdened with wine made from water, alleluia." And on the feast of the Purification, we sing in the processional song: "O Daughter of Sion, adorn thy bridal-chamber, and welcome the King" (*Adorna thalamum tuum*). Christ's being brought to the temple is the visit of the spouse to his bride.

[4] *Concerning Virgins*, VI, 31.

Now Pius XII, in his encyclical on the Mystical Body reminded us in no uncertain terms that the Church, the bride of Christ, was born or came into being, not on Pentecost Day, as had been frequently supposed, but on the Cross (n. 29, 30). This truth, not so easily apparent if the metaphor of the Mystical Body is used, becomes much clearer in terms of the Church as the spouse of Christ. As Eve proceeded from the side of Adam, so the second Eve, the Church, came forth from the pierced side of Christ, the second Adam.

The same thought is moreover very forcefully expounded in the liturgical texts of the feast of the Sacred Heart: "From the pierced heart, the Church, joined or espoused to Christ, is born —*Ex corde scisso, Ecclesia, Christo jugata, nascitur.*" This verse from the Vesper hymn puts in summary, poetic form what was the common outlook of tradition. As witnesses, the greatest and most representative doctors of East and West, Chrysostom and Augustine, are summoned, and their testimony is given in the lessons of the octave of the feast. Augustine: "The second Adam, with bowed head, slept on the cross, that thence might be formed his spouse, which came forth from the side of the sleeping One" (the octave day). And Chrysostom: "For blood and water came forth, because from them the Church is constituted" (i.e., blood and water, symbols of the Eucharist and baptism, are symbols thereby of the Church of the Sacraments. Saturday within the octave). And to indicate that this idea was still prevalent in later centuries, the Church quotes also from St. Lawrence Justinian (d. 1456): "When from the side of the sleeping Adam one of his ribs was taken and from it Eve, the mother of all, was formed, this was a type of the Church. . . . For while the true Adam slept on the cross, from his side, as water and blood flowed forth, was formed the Church, his beautiful bride without spot or wrinkle" (Monday within the octave).

If then the liturgy and the earlier Fathers, especially the Fathers of the East, speak already of the Incarnation of Christ as an espousal, this presupposes, I think, the so-called mystical theory of redemption, or the theory of union. Or we might, with St. Gregory the Great, simply say: "God the Father prepared the nuptials for God the Son when he united the Son to human nature in the womb of the Virgin."[5] The Incarnation, as it were, was the betrothal. And all his subsequent activity meant a winning of the bride unto himself, climaxing in his death on the cross whereby "Christ loved the Church and delivered himself up for her" (Eph. 5:25). And Pentecost? The Church is the bride of Christ: therefore what happened to him she also must experience; what is his belongs also to her. Christ was born at Bethlehem; but at the Jordan the Spirit descended upon him to anoint him for his public mission. So too the Church, though she came into full being on Calvary, had yet to be filled with the Spirit in order to begin her public mission. Christ gave the Spirit, his Spirit, as his dowry to the Church, his bride, on Pentecost Day.

But if we say, as we must, that the Church was born on the cross, that she came forth from the pierced side of Christ, we must not forget that she came forth in full stature, as the bride in all her beauty and strength whom the Son of God came down from heaven to win for himself. And the spousal union is a union of love, a union of life: of mind and heart. It is not, as it was in the Old Testament, a union with a slave girl, but a union with a free woman (Gal. 4:21–31). The covenant, the nuptial contract, he makes with her is not like the covenant God made with the chosen people, on Mount Sinai, a covenant between a master and his handmaid, but a covenant of intimate love (cf. Hebr. 12:18 sq.). Let us call to mind again the Last Supper, when this new and eternal covenant was established in Christ's blood. Let us remember the last discourse, whose whole theme was love, love of Christ for his disciples, his Church, and the need of their love of one another. This new covenant will last until the Spirit will say to the bride, "come," and the bridegroom will present his spouse at the throne of the eternal Father and God will be all in all.

Christ and the Church, spouse and bride, became two in one flesh—became as it were one person. The same intimacy of

---

[5] *In Evangelia*, lib. II, hom. 38, no. 3 (P.L. 76, 1283). The emphasis on the Incarnation in the work of redemption was particularly dear to the seventeenth-century French school of theology: Berulle, Olier, Condren. Scheeben, in his *Mysteries of Christianity*, also gives it considerable prominence.

union is expressed by this metaphor as when St. Paul speaks of Christ and the Church constituting one body. But with the figure of the marriage bond, this intimate union of life is presupposed, and greater stress is placed on the intimacy of love ("Christ loved the Church and delivered Himself up for her"— Eph. 5:25), an intimacy of love that caused the unity of life. It was a love that urged Christ to lift up his spouse from servitude to equality of life with himself; a love that will make the bride reflect most perfectly the mind and heart of the beloved; a love that is life-giving: "that he might sanctify here, . . . that she might be holy and without blemish" (Eph. 5:25-27).

Perhaps it is correct to say that the figure of the spouse and bride is calculated to call more explicit attention to the moral side of Christian life (that is also why St. Paul introduced it in Eph. 5, in order to draw moral consequences about married and family life). For the bride is bound to her spouse in complete fidelity and love, in a whole-souled devotion which does not, and may not, share affection. St. Bernard, with his usual unction, sums up these traits of Church and Christians which her spousal relation entails: purity, obedience, tenderness, devotion, unity of opinion, of love, of interests; the inviolable fidelity of a heart not divided; eagerness to bear abundant good fruits in oneself and to bring souls unto Christ (cf. Anger, *Doctrine of the Mystical Body*, p. 158). And we know to what magnificent heights of the mystical life this spousal relationship, as applied to the individual soul, has led in the history of the Church's saints.

The comparison of the spouse and bride indicates, moreover, more vividly than the Mystical Body metaphor, the fruitfulness of the union, the growth of the Kingdom of God through constantly new members. In so far, therefore, it corresponds more immediately to the parables of the mustard seed, of the leaven, etc., in which the Church's apostolic mission is stressed. The four so-called "marks of the Church" also receive new fullness of meaning in the light of this figure. The Church is "one," because she is united to Christ in bridal love; they are two in one flesh. She is "holy," because she is the bride whom Christ won for Himself on the Cross, whom He sanctified by His blood "that he might present her to himself holy, without spot or wrinkle" (Eph. 5:27). She is "catholic," because Christ by uniting Himself to a human nature in the womb of Mary betrothed Himself to the whole human race; because, by shedding His blood for all men, He espoused his bride on the Cross. She is "apostolic," because it is on the apostles as the first children of the Church, the first members of her family, that the Church is founded.

And finally, if the Church is the bride of Christ, then the Spirit of Christ, the Spirit of holiness, must also be operative in her. As the bride of Christ, she is the temple of the Holy Spirit, who dwells in her as the soul dwells in its own body. He overshadows the bride of Christ as once He overshadowed the womb of Mary, that from the womb of the Church new sons of God may be born.

By way of introduction to succeeding chapters, it will be necessary to add here some basic ideas about how this spousal relationship between Christ and His Church finds application, or rather, is realized anew, in the matrimonial union between Christian husband and wife. Eph. 5 is again our glorious witness to this consoling truth: for St. Paul was addressing Christians, and therefore speaking of Christian matrimony.

"This is a great mystery—I mean in reference to Christ and to the Church" (v. 32). Christian marriage is a great mystery, a great spiritual happening, a holy thing, because it is a living image, a replica, of the great mystery: Christ's union with his bride, the Church. It is rooted in this mystery and is organically connected with it, and so partakes of its nature and sacred character. Christian marriage is not merely a symbol, a figure, of Christ's union with the Church; for then it would not be mysterious at all. It is not an empty symbol, but a living image that reproduces the exemplar. It represents, i.e., re-represents the great mystery of Christ and the Church, because this mystery proves active and operative in it. Christ's union with his Church is the ideal of Christian marriage, yes; but more than that, it is its root. The great mystery of Christ and his bride vibrantly lives, operates and manifests itself in the union of Christian husband and wife. Christian marriage can be called an offshoot, a living branch, of Christ's union with the Church. It grows out of that union, is its extension, replica, and organ. It reproduces and expands the union of Christ and his Church at a particular point, for a particular end: the expansion of that union through new offspring.[6]

Karl Adam expresses this basic concept of Christian matrimony even more graphically:

"The fundamental mystery of Christianity, the nuptial relationship between Christ and his Church as one sole Body, as two in one flesh, is realized anew in every Christian marriage. Wherever Christian bride and bridegroom unite in wedlock, the holy union which exists between the most sacred humanity of Christ and its members receives new actuality. In the eyes of faith, it is not the parents who solely by their own power prepare the body of the members of Christ, but Christ and His Church beget through their agency."[7]

What St. Paul says to all: "Know you not that your bodies are the members of Christ? . . . Or know you not that your members are the temple of the Holy Ghost? . . . and you are not your own" (I Cor. 6:15–20), can be applied with special relevance to Christian parents: you are not your own. You belong to Christ and his bride, who desire to make use of you to bring new sons of God into the world. The Christian husband does not belong to his wife, nor the wife to her husband, as much as they both belong to Christ and his Church, as their instruments—for the purpose of making the union between Christ and his Church fruitful, for the purpose of increasing the family of God unto his greater glory.

When therefore a Christian man and woman unite in holy marriage, they not only assume obligations toward each other and their expected offspring, but they dedicate themselves to God for a holy service, the extension of his kingdom among men.[8] They are to bring into the world, not only children as images of God (every marriage has that end), but to beget adorers in spirit and in truth. Christ and the Church, his bride,

---

[6] The paragraph above is borrowed almost verbatim from Scheeben's *Mysteries of Christianity*, pp. 601–604.

[7] "The Sanctification of Marriage," *Orate Fratres*, IX (1934–35), 175.

[8] Scheeben, *op. cit.*, p. 599.

have as their first objective to form a cult community, to praise the Father. So also husband and wife. The family, the home, must become a temple of God, a house of God and a gate of heaven: an *ecclesiola*, as St. John Chrysostom called it.

III. THE LORD'S DAY IN THE OLD AND NEW TESTAMENT

On Sundays, God is in a very special manner the good master of the household of whom Christ told us in the Gospel. He invites us to His house, to be His guests at table: and He gives us generously of His treasures, *nova et vetera*, new and old. New *and old!* There is danger of forgetting or neglecting the old, because the new treasures, the treasures brought us by Christ in the New Dispensation, are so wonderful.

We must consider the old if we wish to have a true understanding of the new. For the old is the foundation of the new; and we must look to the foundation if we want the superstructure to be sound. Christ Himself said: "Do not think that I have come to destroy the law or the prophets. I have not come to destroy, but to fulfill."[1] Thus, e.g., the commandments of the Old Law have not become unimportant just because Christ has in the New Dispensation given us the greater law of love. Sociologists have been warning us that we in America are to a large extent a rootless generation. That could spell tragedy. But to be spiritually rootless constitutes an even greater danger. "Let us look to the rock from which we have been hewn." In our topic of Sunday, and Sabbath too, the words of Pius XI must be properly applied: "Spiritually we are Semites."

I must write first of all, then, of the Sabbath in the Old Testament. It is a vast topic. We meet with the Sabbath for the first time in the history of Exodus, in the account of Moses leading the chosen people out of Egypt. That was roughly 1500 years

Liturgical Week 1949, St. Louis, Mo.
[1] Matt. 5:17.

before Christ; and 1500 years is a long period of time. Obviously therefore in a book such as this, I must limit myself to only a few aspects—those namely which have most significance for our understanding of the Sunday.

We can summarize the divine purpose of God in instituting the Sabbath under two main headings:

1) The Sabbath is a memorial of *creation*.

2) The Sabbath is a sign of the *Covenant* that God established with the Jewish people.

Only secondarily, only derivatively (no matter how uppermost it may have been in the minds of the people and stressed in practice), was the Sabbath a day of rest, i.e., a day of cessation from work.

This meaning was particularly emphasized by God when He gave Moses the Ten Commandments and thereby for the first time commanded the Jews to observe the Sabbath. The account is contained in Exodus, chapter 20:

I am the Lord thy God. . . . Remember that thou keep *holy* the Sabbath day. Six days shalt thou labor, and shalt do all thy works. But on the seventh day is the Sabbath of the Lord thy God: Thou shalt do no work on it, thou nor thy son, nor thy daughter, nor thy manservant nor thy maidservant, nor thy beast, nor the stranger that is within thy gates. *For* in six days the Lord made heaven and earth, and the sea, and all things that are in them, and rested on the seventh day; *therefore* the Lord blessed the seventh day and sanctified it.

The seventh day, accordingly, is a day *holy unto the Lord,* because it is the day that celebrates the completion of the work of creation. Hence, too, the commandment of the Sabbath belonged to the first of the two tablets of the Ten Commandments: that is, it is concerned with man's direct obligations to God. The Sabbath is a sacred day, set aside for God, consecrating to God a definite period of time. It is the day of memorial, the day which the Jews must dedicate to Him who said: "I am the Lord your God," i.e., your Creator. God Himself, therefore, set aside a special day on which He commanded His people to honor Him in a special manner.

And this furnishes us with our first profound spiritual lesson. At first glance it may seem a paradox that God should so set aside a special day dedicated to Himself. For if man's relation to God means anything, it means that he is totally and absolutely dependent on Him every moment of his life. Man's very existence, all that he is and has, is from God, is a gift from God. Man's recognition of this total dependence should accordingly be constant. His *internal* worship, in other words, cannot be truthfully limited to set places and times.[2]

But *outward manifestation* of this internal worship is another matter. To put it most simply: man cannot be continuously occupied, externally, with worshipping God; he must be about the work of earning his daily bread. St. Thomas adds another, more spiritual reason. He reminds us that the chief purpose of external divine cult is that men might have a greater reverence for God.[3] But man is so constituted that he has less respect, or pays less honor, to common everyday things, to things that are not set aside in some way. That the mind of man might be stirred to greater reverence for the majesty of God, certain objects have therefore been set aside in an especial manner for Him—although *all* things are really His. Thus there are sacred persons, sacred places, sacred vessels, and sacred days and seasons, ordained for the external worship of God.

Such "segregation" unto God is all the more necessary when there is question of external *public, social* worship. An individual's life can be a constant walking in the divine presence; a community, however, can meet together for public worship only at intervals, at stated times. Hence specially consecrated or sacred days are essential in terms of the religious life of a *community*, rather than of the individual. And the very fact that God instituted the sacred day of Sabbath argues that He was commanding *community* worship. This is moreover explicitly stated by God when, later, He ordered which days were to be kept holy. First in the list is the Sabbath:

"And the Lord spoke to Moses, saying: Speak to the children of Israel, and say to them. These are the feasts of the Lord *on which you will gather in sacred assemblies*: these are my feasts.

[2] Hence Christ's command to "pray always"; hence the insistent urging of every spiritual writer to "walk in the presence of God."
[3] *Summa Theologica*, I–II, q. 102.

Six days shall you work, but the seventh will be a sabbath of complete rest *with a holy assembly;* you shall do no work on it, for it is a day of rest, consecrated to God in whatever place you may live."[4]

All this does not mean, however, that dedicating *a* sacred day to God leaves the other days unholy: or that by giving *one* day to God man can thereby reserve the other six entirely to himself. It is not just giving God a part of your life. Rather, by giving Him a part in this special and solemn manner, you express your intention of giving Him the whole. The part stands for the whole—as in the case of offering God the first fruits of the harvest, or the tithes. The part stands for the whole, and thereby implicitly consecrates the whole.

To summarize: the Sabbath was a solemn recognition by the Jewish community and by all its members that God had sovereign rights: "I am the Lord your God." It was a public admission that *all* comes from Him, that He is their Lord and Creator. As a memorial day of creation, the Jewish Sabbath meant a worship of *adoration* ("I am the Lord your God, you shall not have strange gods before me"); a worship of *total submission;* and it was likewise a worship of *thanksgiving* for all His goodness, all His gifts to them, a thanksgiving, i.e., for all they were and had.

From this viewpoint, too, we can now the better understand the inner significance of the *rest* commanded by God. Servile work, laborious and burdensome work, is a result of our first parents' sin: "In the sweat of thy brow thou shalt eat thy bread. . . . Cursed be the earth in thy work." Man, as the image of God, was to have *dominion* over creatures. By sin, which means a preferring of creatures to God, man became a slave to these creatures: these, in spite of themselves, achieved dominion over man. Man's weekly work, therefore, is a constant reminder, a "hang-over" of his sin, of his lack of submission to God. And at the same time, insofar as man becomes absorbed with creatures, his weekly life and work constitute a constant *danger* of again being drawn away from God. The Sabbath rest from work, a rest

[4] Lev. chapter 23.

from absorbing concern with creatures, meant getting a proper perspective again of creatures in their relation to the Creator. It was a day for man to say to God: You alone are the true Ruler, I am but your steward. It was a day of truth, of being realistic, a day of taking stock, of rooting themselves anew in God. Adapting a famous phrase of St. Augustine, we might say that the Jews on the Sabbath learned to pray: "Our hearts are (or, should be) restless all week, until they today rest again in Thee, O God."

And God knows it is a lesson we in the New Testament, and especially in these days, and in our own country, with its all-absorbing spirit of materialism and secularism, are desperately in need of ourselves.

The Sabbath then was the memorial of creation. And consequently, it was the type, the forerunner, the foreshadowing of the Sunday of the New Testament, which is the memorial of re-creation, of the new creation granted us by Christ. The Sabbath was the day when God was honored as the author and Master of man's natural life. The Sunday is the day when we rejoice in the gift of the new, divine life—the very possibility of which was unknown to the Jews. Celebrating the Sunday, however, we should not forget its foundation, the Sabbath. The Church herself does not fail to remind us: "O God, who in a wonderful way didst establish the human race (Sabbath), and more wonderfully didst re-form it (Sunday). . . ." (Offertory of the Mass.)

Besides being a memorial of creation, we said at the outset that the Sabbath was likewise a memorial of the Covenant by which God made the Jews His chosen race. It was to be a perpetual memorial of their liberation from the slavery of Egypt. This is the meaning of the Sabbath which God stressed most when He gave the commandments to Moses the second time:

"Observe the day of the Sabbath, to sanctify it. . . . Six days shalt thou labor and shalt do all thy works. The seventh is the day of the Sabbath, that is the rest of the Lord thy God. Thou shalt not do any work therein, thou, nor thy sons, nor thy daughter, nor thy manservant. . . . *Remember that thou also didst serve in Egypt, and the Lord thy God brought thee out from thence with a strong hand,* and a stretched-out arm. *Therefore* hath he commanded thee that thou shouldst observe the Sabbath day."[5]

Again, when God delivered to Moses the two tablets of stone with the Commandments, He instructed him, saying:

"Speak to the children of Israel, and thou shalt say to them: See that you keep my Sabbath; *because it is a sign* between me and you in your generations. . . . Keep you my Sabbath, for it is holy unto you. . . . Let the children of Israel keep the Sabbath, and celebrate it in their generations. *It is an everlasting covenant* between me and the children of Israel, and *a perpetual sign.*"[6]

Every Sabbath, therefore, was as it were a solemn *renewal of the Covenant* between God and His *people,* between God and the *community* of the Jewish race. Every Sabbath the people renewed their *dedication* of themselves to His service. Every Sabbath they rejoiced again in the promise of God on Mount Sinai: "If therefore you will hear my voice, and keep my covenant, you shall be my peculiar possession above all people: And you shall be to me a priestly kingdom and a holy nation."[7] (And because observance of the Sabbath was a sign of national loyalty to their divine King, violation of the Sabbath was treason, to be punished by death.)

Hence also, as a sign of the Covenant, of their deliverance from Egypt, the Sabbath logically demanded *rest,* or cessation from work. Their slavery in Egypt had meant *forced* labor, slave labor: a terrible burden. Observing rest on the Sabbath was an act of thanksgiving, an act of worship: for it was an act of public recognition of God's goodness to them, freeing them from that labor of slaves which is so burdensome.

Again we see, therefore, that *rest* was not primary in the Sabbath observance. It was supplementary to worship, it was itself a form of worship. Worship, community worship, was the important element of the Sabbath.

As a sign of the Covenant, the Sabbath had, moreover, the same purpose as the annual celebration of the Pasch, which like-

[5] Deut. 5:15.
[6] Exod. 31:13-17.
[7] Exod. 19:6.

wise celebrated the liberation from the slavery of Egypt. "The Pasch was the great annual Sabbath, and the Sabbath was the weekly, miniature Pasch." (Anticipating a bit, we can already see their counterpart, or rather, their fulfillment, in the New Testament: Easter is our Pasch; Sunday is the weekly Pasch, or the weekly little Easter.) Sabbath and Pasch went hand in hand; and on both occasions the "priestly kingdom, the holy nation" gathered in "holy assembly" to thank and praise their God who had chosen them as His own. Only in the times after the Exile did this spiritual and primary purpose of the Sabbath become obscured, and attention became concentrated on the secondary aspect, the abstention from work. From that time derived all the rigoristic, man-made additions and prescriptions which made the Sabbath a heavy burden, leading to nervous scrupulosity—the kind of Sabbath against which Christ protested so strongly.

Earlier, the Sabbath was not such a blue-law affair, which found its perpetuation and Christian counterpart, e.g., in the seventeenth-century Calvinist Sunday in Scotland, or the Puritan Sunday in New England. We read, for instance, in the Code of Connecticut:

"No one shall run on the Sabbath day, or walk in his garden, or elsewhere, except reverently to and from meeting. No one shall travel, cook victuals, make beds, sweep house, cut hair or shave on the Sabbath. No woman shall kiss her child on the Sabbath. . . . If any man shall kiss his wife, or wife her husband on the Lord's day, the party in fault shall be punished at the discretion of the court of magistrates."

On the contrary, Isaias speaks of the Sabbath as a *day of delight*. Fasting and mourning were forbidden. Special festive white clothes were to be worn. From early times, too, joyous music played a large part in the Sabbath observance.

Nor was the feasting restricted to the Temple—or later, to the Synagogue. It was, and has remained, a great feast of the *home*; so much so, that a modern Jewish writer considers the Sabbath the chief foundation of the remarkably good home life and close family spirit that has characterized Jews through the centuries.[8] All the members of the family were to be present,

[8] A. E. Millgram, *Sabbath. The Day of Delight*, Philadelphia, p. 8.

and, *nota bene*, inviting guests, especially the poor or strangers, or travellers, was a normal custom.[9]

The feast started at sundown of the eve of the Sabbath, with the mother of the family ceremoniously lighting the candles. Then the father, after saying grace over a cup of wine, laid his hand on the head of each of his children, solemnly blessing them with a beautiful prayer.[10] And the meal itself, of course, was especially good, with its own special foods.[11] In fact, some Rabbis taught that the Sabbath should be equally divided, half of it being devoted to reading the Law, the other half to eating and drinking joyfully. The same Jewish writer whom we just quoted states: "These and other Sabbath observances not only hallowed the Sabbath but also sanctified the Jewish home, making it a *Mikdash Me'at*, a miniature sanctuary, in which the parents were the priests and the family table was the altar."[12] And it was God Himself who had linked the Sabbath observance with filial piety: "Ye shall fear every man his mother and his father, and ye shall keep my sabbaths: I am the Lord your God."[13]

At the time of Christ, this joyful, spiritual, worshipful aspect of the Sabbath, which the prophets had constantly stressed, had become obscured. It had become a day of superstitious legalism, a matter of rigoristic external observance of the law of *rest*. The means had become an end.

Christ Himself observed the Sabbath, to give an example of obedience. But His interpretation of it, *in practice*, became a chief source of His conflict with the Pharisees. With the prophets of old, He insisted that not physical rest, but the spiritual content of the Sabbath is the more important. And hence, since He came to bring the new law of love of God and neighbor,

[9] Christ accepted such an invitation in the home of the Pharisee. Cf. Luke 14:1.

[10] If Jewish parents could in the Old Testament bless their children with the assurance that thereby God was blessing them, how much more should Christian parents adopt this custom: for the New Testament is the fulfillment of the Old! There is a wonderful power of blessing in the hands of Catholic parents. May they learn to use it!

[11] "Gefilte fish" was originally a Sabbath delicacy.

[12] *Loc. cit.*

[13] Lev. 19:3.

He repeatedly healed the sick on a Sabbath day: He declared Himself Lord of the Sabbath—and mercy and love are of the soul of interior worship in the Messianic era.

Over against the slavish observance of the Old Testament, He brought the *liberty* of the true sons of God. This liberty, this liberation from the slavery of sin to which the Old Testament was still subject, He established by His blessed passion and death, which He freely took upon Himself on the eve of the Sabbath. And providentially, the eve of the Sabbath that year was likewise the eve of the Pasch. His death marked the death of both Sabbath and Pasch. But it was also the beginning of the memorial of re-creation, of the memorial of the New Covenant of God with His new Chosen People!

On the morning after the Sabbath (so the Evangelist tells us) Christ rose from the dead. On this day, which we now call Sunday (but which the Russians still call "Resurrection"), He appeared to His disciples and gave them the gift of the sacrament of penance. Seven days later, again on a Sunday, the apostles were gathered together, this time with Thomas the Doubter. And again Christ stood in their midst, and gave Thomas the gift of deepened faith. This day after the Sabbath, this day of Sunday, evidently was something special. The apostles began to look upon it as the day of meeting their risen Lord, a day of spiritual joy and favor. And hence it could hardly have come as a surprise to them that when the risen Christ chose to give them His greatest gift, His own Spirit, it was again on a Sunday, the Sunday of Pentecost, that He did so.

Sunday, therefore, came to mean *the day of living contact with the risen Christ;* it became the weekly day of joyfully celebrating His memory with the memorial He Himself had left them: the Holy Eucharist. In the early history of the Church, as described for us in the writings of the New Testament, the Sunday's meaning can then be briefly summarized as the day on which the community of Christians celebrated the memory of the risen Lord by celebrating together the Sacrament of Thanksgiving. It was, as St. John in the Apocalypse first called it, the "Lord's Day," because on it, to quote St. Paul,[14] the Lord's

14 I Cor., chapter 11.

Supper was partaken of. On the Sabbaths of old, the loaves of proposition were changed, lest they corrupt. Sunday in the New Dispensation is the day on which the Bread of Life confers upon His people incorruption. And since Sunday was the day of meeting the risen Lord, no wonder that at their Sunday Eucharistic gatherings the early Christians also looked forward in a particular manner to their final meeting with Him, at His second and glorious coming.[15]

I shall add, in conclusion, what I think is an important lesson we can learn from the Sabbath for our better observance of the Sunday. Surely, the Sabbath as Sabbath has been abrogated. St. Paul leaves us in no doubt about it in his Epistle to the Colossians, 2:16. But we dare not ignore Pius XI's words: "We are spiritually Semites." Else we run the risk of distorting our spiritual vision, of stunting our spiritual growth. The *lessons* of the Sabbath observance have not been abrogated, but fulfilled, completed, by the spiritual lessons of Sunday.

IV. THE CHURCH YEAR IN ACTION

The holy sacrifice of the Mass is the unbloody renewal of the sacrifice of the Cross. This is a cardinal truth of the Catholic faith: a profound truth, that summarizes in itself as it were the entire glad tidings of our salvation. Hence the Church has not hesitated to insert, among the very words of institution which are the words of consecration, the phrase: *mysterium fidei*. It is not merely *a* mystery of faith, but can rightly be called *the* mystery of faith. Christ's death on the cross is directly signified by the sacramental sign: the *separate* consecration of bread and

Liturgical Week 1958, Cincinnati, Ohio.

[15] I Cor., 11:26: "For as often as you shall eat this bread and drink the cup, you proclaim the death of the Lord, *until he comes*." Cf. the *Didache*, chapter 10, which describes the Eucharistic celebration: "If any man be holy, let him come [and receive] . . . Maranatha [i.e., Our Lord, Come!] Amen."

wine into the sacred Body and Blood of Christ symbolizes and makes present in sacrament the separation of His Body and Blood on the Cross, i.e., His death.

Great is this mystery. But let us not, for very wonder at its greatness, fail to recognize its yet vaster dimensions, that open up to the eyes of faith. The death of Christ is inseparable from His resurrection; it is unthinkable without His resurrection. "He was delivered up for our sins, and rose again for our justification" (Rom. 4:25). Death was His gateway to life, a new and glorious life. His death and resurrection are, of their very nature, but one mystery: the new Pasch, the transition, from Good Friday to Easter Sunday morning.

The celebration of His death, therefore, involves also the celebration of His resurrection. The Mass is the memorial of His death directly, but implicitly and necessarily of His rising from death as well. The resurrection is the mystery of life-giving death brought to its glorious conclusion. The Mass is the sacramental renewal of our redemption, of the mystery of the Cross which was climaxed on the third day when our Saviour triumphed over death and sin.

The Mass is the memorial of Christ's death *and* resurrection. Such has been the faith of the Church from the very outset. This explains the fact that Sunday, that is to say, the day of His resurrection, was chosen as the day on which to celebrate the Holy Eucharist. It explains too why Easter was the first feast to be specially observed, and to be celebrated by means of holy Mass. This conviction, of holy Mass being the memorial of resurrection as well as death, found literary expression moreover in the very first text that has come down to us, of what we would now call the canon: it is found in the *Apostolic Tradition* of St. Hippolytus of Rome, written about the year 215. Christ at the first Eucharistic celebration had said: "For as often as you shall eat this bread and drink this cup, you proclaim the death of the Lord, until he comes" (1 Cor. 11:26). And further: "This is my body which shall be given up for you; do this in remembrance of me" (1 Cor. 11:24). He himself, therefore, refers directly only to His saving death. And yet, the Church, certainly as early as St. Hippolytus, and to our own day, immediately after quoting Christ's words, "Do this in remembrance of me," infallibly interprets these words for us: "Wherefore, mindful *not only* of His blessed passion, *but also of His resurrection* from the grave . . . offer unto Thy majesty . . ."

Mass is the "total work of our redemption" (*totum opus redemptionis*) reenacted. Death and resurrection, we have said, constitute the one completed act of redemption, which is made operative for us in the Mass. "He died for our sins, and rose again for our justification." But we must widen our vision of the Mass, the Mystery of Faith, yet more, if we wish to understand its true dimensions.

The prayer after consecration, which we just quoted, speaks not only of death and resurrection but mentions also the ascension; and in other times, and in Eastern rites as well, further mysteries of Christ's life have been and are enumerated: His birth, His baptism in the Jordan, even His final coming. These too, and in fact, all acts of Christ's life, are part of the mystery of redemption, are present as the cause of our salvation in every celebration of holy Mass. The famous secret of the Ninth Sunday after Pentecost summarily states: "As often as this saving Victim is offered up, it is the work of redemption that is being accomplished."

Pius XII in *Mediator Dei* speaks therefore of the "effrontery" of those who claim that in the liturgy we must see only the glorified Christ in heaven, and not the historical Christ. Rather, "the sacred liturgy presents (*proponit*) to us Christ whole and entire, in all the phases of his life: the Christ who is the Word of the eternal Father, who is born of the Virgin Mother of God, who teaches us truth, who heals the sick and consoles the afflicted, who suffers, and dies; who then triumphs over death by His resurrection, and from His throne in the glory of heaven sends down upon us the Spirit, the Paraclete, to live forever in his Church" (162–163).

In every Mass, consequently, we celebrate not merely our Saviour's death and resurrection, but also *all* His redeeming acts: the *"totum opus,"* the total work of redemption. Every Mass, no matter what the season of the year, is a memorial of the incarnation, of Christ's birth, of Cana, of His baptism, His miracles, His teaching, His deeds and words and prayer, besides His passion and rising in which all these other acts are fulfilled.

All these redemptive acts of Christ are not merely commemorated, or called to mind, in every Mass, but are somehow present and operative, and the present causes of our salvation.

This our third point brings us to the crux of the theological problem of the liturgical year. The big arguments started more than thirty years ago. By now, the air has been somewhat cleared, and although there is as yet no agreement about *how* the historical redemptive events of Christ's life can be presently active and operative, the fact that they are somehow present is being recognized and more generally accepted. Chiefly responsible for this spiritually very important realization are the clear statements of Pius XII in *Mediator Dei*:

"The liturgical year," he writes, "is no cold and lifeless representation of past events, no mere historical record. Rather, it is Christ himself, living on in His Church, and still pursuing that path of boundless mercy which, 'going about and doing good,' He began to tread during his life on earth. This He *does* in order to bring the souls of men into contact with His mysteries, and so make them live by them. These *mysteries are now constantly present and active;* . . . for each of them is, according to its nature and in its own way, the cause of our salvation" (165).[1]

This critically important declaration of Pius XII regarding the present activity of Christ and his mysteries in the liturgical year is a striking instance of what I believe to be the central and most significant message of this entire monumental encyclical. In *Mediator Dei*, Pope Pius XII once and for all put an end to what might be called the divorce between Christ and his Church in Catholic thinking. To put it in perhaps over-simplified terms: Christ did not merely by His life and death merit graces for us, which have as it were been stored up, and which the Church, succeeding Christ in time, now distributes to her children through the sacraments. *Mediator Dei* insists above all, again and again, on the presence and activity of Christ Himself in the liturgical acts:

[1] For the translation of this crucial text, I have used the original Latin, together with the Italian version which appeared in *Osservatore Romano* on Dec. 1, 1947, the day after it published the document in Latin.

"Along with the Church, therefore, her divine Founder is present at *every* liturgical function: Christ is present at the august sacrifice of the altar . . . He is present in the sacraments . . . He is present, finally, in the prayer and petition we direct to God (i.e., official prayer) . . . The liturgy, in short, is the worship rendered by the Mystical Body of Christ in the entirety of its Head and members" (21).

Again: The liturgy is the present exercise of the priesthood of Christ, for "the priesthood of Jesus Christ is a living and continuous reality through all the ages to the end of time" (21).

And even more succinctly: "Christ acts each day to save us" (29).

The mysteries of the liturgical year, therefore, are not just so many didactic opportunities which the Church uses to recall the events of Christ's life, for our edification and imitation. They are "ever present and active," and, to quote the N.C.W.C. translation, "each mystery brings its own special grace for our salvation" (165). "Jesus Christ, yesterday and today, and the same forever" (Heb. 13:8). To quote *Mediator Dei* once again in this context: By these mysteries "we can receive from Him living vitality as branches do from the tree and members from the head; thus slowly and laboriously we can transform ourselves 'unto measure of the age of the fulness of Christ'" (165).[2]

Since, as Pope Pius XII tells us, "the liturgical year is Christ himself, continuing that journey which He began in his mortal life, going about doing good," we can understand immediately why a liturgical feast by its very nature is meant to be a celebration of an *event*, rather than of an abstract idea, or of a dogmatic fact. Hence, to cite an obvious instance, the feast of Pentecost is not a feast of the Holy Ghost, a feast to honor Him as the Third Person of the Trinity. It is a redemptive feast of Christ, sending us His Spirit to complete his saving work.

[2] Three recent studies have considerably contributed to clarification of the manner in which Christ's redemptive mysteries are present and operative in the sacraments: *Die Eucharistie in der Zeit der Griechischen Väter*, by Johnnes Betz, (Freiburg: Herder, 1955); *Le Mystère liturgique d'apres saint Leon le Grand*, by B. de Soos (Paris: Editions du Cerf, 1958); and *Heilsgegenwart*, by Polycarp Wegenaer (Muenster: Aschendorffsche Verlagsbuchhandlung, 1957).

Putting on Christ. Because in the liturgical year "Christ Himself continues that path of boundless mercy which he began to tread during his life on earth, in order to bring souls into contact with his mysteries and so make them live by them," it follows that the Church year is indeed, as it has often been called, our primary school of sanctity. Christ is present and active in our midst, uniting us to the successive mysteries of His redemptive life and action and teaching. All other so-called schools of spirituality, whether Salesian, Jesuit, Franciscan, Benedictine (if there be such), however valid and sound, can only be secondary and implementary to this school of Christian life which is nothing less than the life of Christ himself.

At the same time, we may not apply quantitative, or mathematical, measuring rods to the activity of Christ. We must not label Christ's acts, say, from one to fifty, each of which has its special grace, and then conclude that one must be united to all of them in order to live with Christ, or to be like Christ: that missing one means missing this particular aspect of Christ's holiness.

If that were true, then centuries of Christianity were very unChrist-like, because the liturgical year developed its feasts and seasons only very gradually. It would mean, for instance, that for at least three hundred years, Christians did not experience the grace of Christ's nativity. Each Mass contains the *totum opus,* the full sum of Christ's mysteries; their unfolding through the liturgical year, according to specific feasts and propers, does not mean isolating each one successively. It is Christ, the author of all grace, who is active in each mystery; the same Christ who with a mere look and the words, "Come, follow me," caused Andrew and Peter to follow Him to their own deaths on the cross. Every word of Christ, to use the description customarily applied to the Eucharist, "contains in itself all sweetness." The spiritual life is not a series of neatly labelled packages, the sum of which constitutes sanctity. The intensity of charity, the soul of all virtues, is decisive; and each act of Christ is capable of producing charity in heroic degree, whether that expresses itself in poverty, humility, chastity, or any other virtue.

Thus, while each feast, each Mass, may have its own special grace, the result on the part of the recipient may be as varied as human souls are varied and have their own varied spiritual needs. I am sure that, even historically, the same birth of Christ had quite different effects upon the Magi, the shepherds, and other visitors from Bethlehem, not to speak of Mary and Joseph. And the same sermon on the mount, how vastly varied will have been its results historically, and how varied likewise the effects now, when Christ in the midst of His family speaks it through His minister on All Saints Day!

But the point needs no belaboring. One may merely recall how many different interpretations the Fathers of the Church have given to identical incidents in the Gospels, in their homilies; or how multiple the interpretations of the same Gospel text on thousands of pulpits every Sunday; or how one liturgical commentator, e.g., Father Parsch, differs from the next, e.g., Abbot Baur. And each may have a valid and useful interpretation. It does not matter. They are merely aids. What does matter is that each soul be open to the words of Christ, and whether it be like a sturdy oak that requires buckets of water or like a blade of grass that needs only a few drops, that it humbly accept the rain of divine grace which God's mercy sends, and collaborate with it.

This view of things will also be helpful when, for instance in the Sundays after Pentecost, the Mass propers have no unified theme. The gospels of that season were chosen quite independently of the epistles, the introits again have their own successive series, and so have the graduals. It doesn't matter. For it is Christ who speaks to us each Sunday, in both Old and New Testament texts, and each word of His can be like the "Come, follow me" that drew Peter and Andrew irrevocably.

Nevertheless, because of our human weakness, which is all too liable to be bored upon hearing the same familiar texts year after year, there is merit in the hope of many liturgists for a three- or four-year cycle of Scripture readings especially for the Sundays of the year. Even in the first centuries, when there were very few feasts, the Christians did have the advantage of the *lectio continua*, the continuous reading of Sacred Scripture, the full message of Christ.

Though the liturgical year brings us into living contact with the mysteries of Christ's life, each of which has its special grace, every Mass is first and foremost the reenactment of the supreme mystery of His death and resurrection. Death and life are the cardinal mysteries, or rather, Mystery. All that preceded in Christ's life led up to this one greatest Mystery, were already partial expressions of it, and are contained in it, are fulfilled by it. From the moment of His incarnation, Christ was High Priest: "In the head of the book it is written of me: Behold, I come to do thy will" (Heb. 10:7). Every deed He performed, every breath He took, every word He spoke was a doing of the will of the heavenly Father. It was all a dying to self, and a corresponding living unto the Father, climaxed by Cross and resurrection.

We might say, therefore, that every mystery of Christ's redemptive life realized already to a partial degree His death and resurrection. Each act of His was already death and resurrection in anticipation, in miniature.

If, then, in the mysteries of the liturgical year, we put on Christ, in every case it must be, in some form or other, a dying to self in order to live more perfectly to God. Whatever the grace of each feast, it has this unvarying substratum. In every Mass, we must (to quote John the Baptist) decrease, that Christ may increase. Such is the necessary pattern of Christ's holiness in us. Death and life comprise all.

May I venture to suggest here that we might profitably carry over this lesson to our descriptions of the spiritual life generally? The terminology that speaks of the purgative, illuminative, and unitive ways has been canonized by long and fruitful usage; but in its origins it was an attempt to baptize Gnostic and Neoplatonic categories. Viewed more closely, these three so-called "ways" can moreover be reduced to terms of death and life: the purgative means dying to sin and self; the illuminative and unitive signify progressive degrees of living for God and with God. I am not suggesting that these terms be discarded. But I do believe that these terms are too formidable for general use; that they are apt to give the impression that the spiritual life can be understood only by an elite. And they do, or are apt to, distract from the simplicity and urgency of the perfection which is meant for all, and which is contained fully in Christ's death and resurrection, and in our consequent dying to self and living unto God. St. Gertrude, by the way, is a luminous example of one who attained the highest degree of mystical union by living the various phases of Christ's mystery of death and life in the liturgical year.

To show that the liturgical year has a didactic purpose, that is, that it teaches us about God and His economy of salvation as realized in Christ, and that it teaches in a most effective manner, it will suffice to recall the declaration of Pope Pius XI, in his encyclical *Quas primas* of December 11, 1925, on Christ the King:

"People are better instructed in the truths of faith and brought to appreciate the interior joys of religion far more effectively by the annual celebration of the sacred mysteries than by even the weightiest pronouncements of the teaching Church. For such pronouncements reach only the few, and these generally the more learned, whereas all the faithful are stirred and taught by the celebration of the feasts; pronouncements speak only once; celebrations speak annually, and as it were continuously; pronouncements affect the mind primarily; celebrations have a salutary influence on the mind and heart, i.e., on the whole man."

We might add for good measure Pius XII's statement, made exactly ten years and a day later: "The liturgy is not the teaching of this or that particular person, but the teaching of the Church . . . The liturgy is the most important organ of the ordinary magisterium of the Church."

Nevertheless, however effective and authoritative the liturgical texts may be in teaching, it may be argued that teaching is their purpose only indirectly. Their all-embracing purpose is life: communication of divine life, in order that God's people may the more worthily worship him in union with Christ.

Mediator Dei expresses this hierarchy of values clearly: "In thus reminding the faithful of these mysteries of Jesus Christ, the sacred liturgy seeks to make them share them in such a way that the divine Head of the Mystical Body lives by his perfect holiness in each of his members" (152). The liturgical year, in other words, seeks to give that knowledge which *is* life, according to the words of Christ himself at the Last Supper: "Now this is everlasting life, that they may know thee, the only true God, and him whom thou hast sent, Jesus Christ" (John 16:3).

We might formulate all this by saying: the liturgical year is didactic, not directly but indirectly; directly, its purpose even in teaching is to deepen faith, hope, and charity in God's holy people. And it does so, or rather, is meant to do so, by its very celebration. What do I mean by that?

We have come to associate faith, hope, and charity rather exclusively with certain prayer acts performed by individuals: the so-called acts of faith, hope, and charity, which every child learns as essential elements of its prayer life. As a matter of fact, such prayer-acts, and the emphasis placed on them, are a catechetical device, deriving only from the sixteenth century. They are, in origin, definitions of faith, hope, and charity put into prayer form. There can be no question, of course, that they are important, spiritually very useful. But this predominant association with the individual has to some extent made us lose sight of the fact that faith, hope, and charity are essential characteristics, life-currents, of the Church first of all. She is the bride of Christ, the *columna veritatis,* the pillar of truth, to whom Christ has committed His revelation; she it is who is journeying through the centuries on hopeful pilgrimage to her heavenly home; it is in her that Christ's love is centered and contained for all to share. Faith, hope, and charity are not just formulas for her, not even prayer formulas. Every time she offers the Eucharistic Mysteries of her Lord, throughout the liturgical year, it is her great act of faith in the redemptive passion and resurrection of Christ: *mysterium fidei.* Every Mass is the joyous expression of her sure hope that her task will be crowned by the eternal liturgy in heaven, with which this celebration brings her, even now, into living contact. Every Eucharist is by definition the sacrifice and sacrament of charity, by which her children are united to Christ and to one another. Prepared by the instructions and prayers of Mass, we, too, are swept forward in this great current of the Church's faith, hope, and charity—"whose faith is known to thee, and whose devotion manifest" —we *act* our faith, hope, and charity in the most eminent and perfect manner, and do not merely formulate them.

Didactic the Eucharistic texts most certainly are; but not in any limited catechetical sense of gaining more information about Christ and His works. St. Paul did not say: "Learning from hearing," but "*faith* from hearing"; and he was referring to the reading of the word of God and the preaching that took place in the framework of holy Mass.

What St. Thomas says about the triple signification of every sacrament can and should be applied correspondingly also to the Church year. Past, present, and future coalesce into a grace-laden unity of divine mercy every time the holy sacrifice is celebrated. To quote Pius XII again, from *Mediator Dei*: we "come into contact with his (historical) mysteries and live by them" (i.e., the Church year not only signifies, but effectively signifies, the past: the redemptive actions of Christ). These mysteries are still now constantly present and active ". . . since each of them is, according to its nature and in its own way, the cause of our salvation" (i.e., the Church year effectively signifies *present* grace conferred). And thirdly, every Mass is an effective *sursum corda*, "a magnificent hymn of praise offered by the Christian family through Jesus, its perpetual advocate, to the heavenly Father" (i.e., every Mass puts us into living contact with the liturgy and its eternal High Priest in heaven; it is a sharing, *communicantes*, with our family at the throne of God, with the angels in whose eternal *Sanctus* we are here and now privileged to join). To use St. Thomas' terminology, the liturgical year "is a commemorative sign of what has gone before, I mean the passion of Christ; and a demonstrative sign of what is being brought about in us through the passion of Christ, that is, grace; and a prognostic, that is, a prophetic sign, of the future glory" (*Summa Theologica, III*, q. 60, a. 3).

This interpretation of the sacraments, and especially of the Eucharist as it is celebrated concretely in the liturgical year, is, I might almost say, commonplace—even though, in practice, attention was riveted almost exclusively on the present signification, namely of grace here and now conferred, until the liturgical movement occasioned theologians to investigate more seriously the connotations of past and future significations. (A pioneer in this fuller understanding of the triple signification was Vonier, in his *Key to the Doctrine of the Eucharist*.)

But I wonder whether, in thus trying to do justice to the Eucharist, or to the Church year celebrated in the texts of the Eucharist as an effective *triple* sign, we have done far less than justice to what might be called a *fourth* manner in which the Eucharist signifies. Father Vagaggini, in an important recent book calls it "the obligative sign." Briefly, it is growth in virtue, the moral obligation to live more intimately in Christ, as a result of partaking in this Eucharistic celebration. Every single Mass in its proper as well as its ordinary parts stresses it. The collect and postcommunion especially without fail voice it explicitly: e.g., "Almighty and merciful God, it is through your grace that the faithful are able to serve You fittingly and laudably. *Grant that we may hurry without faltering,* toward the rewards You have promised us." *God's sacramental gift becomes our personal obligation.* Or, putting it another way, action must follow being: plunged more deeply into the saving mysteries of Christ, we must now manifest his life in our actions.

It is all so obvious, that it need merely be mentioned to be recognized as true. But I wonder whether we in the liturgical movement have sufficiently stressed this "fourth sign" as an essential component of the Eucharistic celebration, rather than as a moralizing afterthought. We have, it seems to me, been so concerned to make clear the triple signification which the sacrament has *ex opere operato,* objectively, by the very fact of its celebration, that we have in practice often failed to bring the *ex opere operantis,* the subjective collaboration of the participants, into the picture as vigorously as does the liturgy itself.

The day is past in quite a number of areas, thank God, when the liturgical movement is misunderstood as externalism, as an affair primarily of rubrics and ceremonial pomp and practices. But men of good will are still suspicious of us, because they feel that by our criticism of individualism and our insistence on communal worship, we neglect and even condemn personal piety. One of them has recently stated that the liturgical movement amounts to a Christianized form of Marxist collectivism. And I insist: these are men of good will. They sense a danger which Pius XII in *Mediator Dei* in no uncertain terms castigated: the opposition between what has been called objective, and subjective or personal piety. They are convinced that liturgists pay so much attention to the *ex opere operato,* the objective efficacy of the sacramental sign, that the *ex opere operantis,* the quotient of personal effort, becomes tragically obscured.

If the problem is put in such bald terms, I would for my own part like to go on record to state my conviction that the liturgical movement's chief objective is to guide and direct and encourage a proper *ex opere operantis*. But a *proper,* i.e., appropriate *ex opere operantis*: a personal co-operation based on our understanding of what the sacrament *ex opere operato* accomplishes in us *and* demands of us. And this understanding is precisely what the sacramental sign spells out for us.

Says *Mediator Dei:* "Each Christian soul should be like an altar on which the various phases of the Sacrifice offered by the High Priest are as it were reenacted: the sorrows and tears that remit and expiate sin; the prayer rising up to heaven to God; the self-sacrifice and self-immolation, eager, generous, whole-hearted; the intimate union whereby we commit ourselves and all that is ours to God and find our rest in him: 'The essence of religion is to imitate him whom we worship'" (152).

The liturgical year is indeed a triple sign, of Christ's passion, of present grace, and of future glory; but it is equally, and quite as essentially, a fourth sign, an obligative sign, of effort to realize and manifest in our personal lives, as individuals, and as common members of God's family, that holiness which Christ communicates to us in the sacrament.

And unless we follow the example of the liturgical texts and associate this fourth signification constantly and urgently with the well-known triple sign, as something inseparable from the latter, as something imperatively demanded by the latter (instead of treating it merely as a pious afterthought), the liturgical apostolate may prove guilty of the accusation that it mechanizes, impersonalizes, collectivizes piety.

Even the history of the word *sacrament* teaches us our lesson. The Latin word *sacramentum,* the equivalent of the Greek word *mysterion,* was first used by Tertullian to describe baptism; and *sacramentum* in his time, as he is at pains to make clear, meant the oath of loyalty which the soldier made to his emperor. It had a morally obligative meaning. This fourth signification of the sacramental sign, therefore, is of the essence; it belongs intrinsically. And let not man put asunder, even in the order of instruction, what God has joined.

It has become customary to divide the Church year into two

cycles, called temporal and sanctoral, the first dealing with Christ and his deeds, the second in honor of Mary and the saints. This is a division in our missals, dictated in its origins, it would seem, merely by reasons of convenience, i.e., that the Mass in question could more easily be found—since the first series is governed chiefly by Easter and the succession of Sundays, which do not occur annually on the same date, while the second series is identified with definite dates of the calendar.

I would like to suggest, however, that we have sometimes allowed a merely external, I might say typographical, distinction, to result in a real distinction, and at times in a mental separation. The temporal and sanctoral series have become two parallel *cycles*, and this, I fear has occasioned the less instructed to think of them as two cycles in what amounts to mutual rivalry. There are some people who think more highly of the feast of St. Anthony than they do of Easter. We loosely talk of offering Mass "in honor of St. Kunegunde, or St. Eusebius, etc." I have sometimes idly imagined, rather flippantly perhaps, how embarrassed St. Joseph, for instance, is on his feast day in heaven. Absorbed in adoration of his God, he would be congratulated by his fellow saints on his celebration, and affectionately kidded by them (if such things are allowed up there) about how many Masses are being offered in his honor. In his honor! The very thought of the all-perfect Sacrifice of Christ being offered in his, St. Joseph's, honor, would appear very like appalling blasphemy to the humble saint.

Pope Pius XII in *Mediator Dei* does not speak of two cycles: for him, the liturgical year is one *cycle*, that of Christ. I believe it desirable that we follow his example and cease speaking of two. He writes: "All the year round the celebration of the Eucharistic Sacrifice and the recitation of the divine office revolve, as it were, about the Person of Jesus Christ; the cycle being so contrived as to be wholly dominated by our Saviour in the mysteries of His humiliation, His redemptive work, and His triumph" (151). When he does speak of the feasts of the saints, he says: "Here too the aim of the Church is always to set models before the faithful which may lead them to cultivate in themselves the virtues of the divine Redeemer" (166).

Christ is the Sun that shines and gives light and life in the course of the Church year. The saints do not have an independent light: "For in their virtues there shines forth under different aspects the splendor of Jesus Christ" (167).

This orientation of all toward Christ is abundantly evidenced in the historical development of the feasts of the saints. The first feast of Mary, for instance, was on January 1, the octave day of Christ's nativity: she was honored because she reflected most perfectly in her own person and life the grandeur of her divine Son. For centuries, moreover, no other feasts were known and celebrated except those of martyrs, and other saints whose lives were viewed as living martyrdom: the so-called confessors, virgins, etc. The word *martyr* means witness. They witnessed to none other than Christ. The precious account of the martyr Polycarp, the first evidence we have of a celebration of a saint's feast, with moving eloquence describes how, in honoring Polycarp's bones, the Christians intended above all to worship Christ whose passion was mirrored so remarkably in his saint. As in the litany of the saints, or as in the mosaic processions on the walls of the ancient basilicas, Mary and the men and women saints in the Church year lead us necessarily to the Agnus Dei, who alone takes away the sins of the world.

Mass in honor of St. Joseph, or of St. Bernard? Perhaps we could substitute: Mass with St. Joseph, or with St. Bernard, just as Mass at the old stational churches in Rome was called "*ad sanctum Paulum, ad sanctum Petrum,* etc.*" Undoubtedly, the Church wishes us to venerate their memories ("*memoriam venerantes*"); but their feast day means also, and more importantly, that on this day of the year, we are united with them in a special manner, in holy fellowship ("*communicantes*") helped by them to follow in the footsteps of Christ, and together with them joyously joined in the perfect worship of our common Father *per Christum Dominum nostrum.*

The saints might be compared, as the liturgy sometimes does compare them, to the garment of Christ. And we, like the poor woman with an issue of blood of whom the Gospel tells, touch that garment, strong in faith that it is the power of Christ that flows into us at our touch.

We are sometimes apt to envy the apostles and disciples, and in fact all the contemporaries of Christ in Palestine, for their opportunity of knowing Him, hearing Him, seeing Him, perhaps talking with Him, being friends with Him. We envy their physical intimacy with the Son of God. As a final point to make, I would like to stress emphatically, that had they only known, it was they rather who had every right to envy us. For by means of the liturgical year we are immeasurably closer to Christ than were even His favored apostles Peter, James, and John while walking in the flesh with Him; closer, I am tempted to say, than was the Blessed Virgin herself, until after the descent of the Spirit at Pentecost.

Christ at the Last Supper stated clearly: "It is *expedient* for you that I go; for if I do not go, the Advocate will not come to you" (John 16:7). And of an earlier occasion, commenting on Christ's words, "If anyone thirst, let him come to me and drink," John wrote: "He said this however of the Spirit whom they who believed in him *were* to receive; for the Spirit had not yet been given, since Jesus had not yet been glorified" (John 7:37–39).

Before the glorification of Christ, and more specifically, before the descent of the Spirit, Peter and John knew and loved Christ and lived with Him as friend lives with friend. It was, we might call it, a union of minds and hearts of the natural order. But with the descent of the Spirit, a *completely new dimension* of union was made possible: the sacramental dimension. Through the sacraments, our union with Christ is no longer a mere moral union, of will and sentiment. It is a union of life itself, of actually sharing His life, of being inserted into His very deeds. Through the Eucharist as celebrated in the liturgical year, above all, we live His life.

All of St. Paul's Epistles, for instance, as explained in a previous chapter, have ultimately only this one great good news: we are now "in Christ." Paul was not using figurative language: the union with Christ, he knew, was so intimate that human language and concepts were pitifully inadequate to express it; he was driven to coin new combinations of words, in an effort to at least suggest the reality and closeness of the union.

"I am nailed with Christ to the cross. It is now no longer I that live, but Christ lives in me" (Gal. 2:19). "But God, who is rich in mercy . . . brought us to life together with Christ . . . and raised us up together with him, and seated us together in heaven in Christ Jesus" (Eph. 2:4–6). "For we were buried together with him into death, by means of baptism . . . But if we have died with Christ, we believe that we shall also live together with him" (Rom. 6:4, 8). "For you were buried together with him in baptism, and in him also rose again . . . God, who raised Christ from the dead . . . brought you to life together with him" (Col. 2:12–13). "If therefore you have died together with Christ . . ." (Col. 2:20). "Since therefore you have risen together with Christ, seek the things that are above" (Col. 3:1). I might call attention, in this last quotation, that "seeking the things that are above," i.e., living a virtuous life, does not *constitute* our rising with Christ, but is urged as its logical effect. In other words, the "rising" is not merely something moral. It is something that really happens to us: Christ unites us really to His own rising. How real this rising with Christ is, becomes clear especially in I Cor. 15:13–17. St. Paul does not merely argue that if Christ our Head has risen, then we also, His members, will rise from the dead; he dares to invert the order, saying: "For if the dead do not rise, neither has Christ risen."

Always, you will note, there is question of dying and rising: of Christ's death and resurrection, the great paschal Mystery, which becomes our Mystery, into which we are inserted, by means of every sacrament, but especially by means of the Eucharist, the sum and source of all sacraments. This concentration then is as it were unfolded for our sake into its component parts: and thus we put on Christ from day to day, Sunday to Sunday, year after year. More correctly, it is He who in the sacrament puts us on. And then it is our obligation and privilege to manifest Him and His activities and virtues in our daily living.

As Pius XII said in *Mediator Dei*: "This requires of us also an earnest and powerful effort and unremitting practice, that we may imitate the mysteries of his life, follow willingly in the way of his sufferings, and so at last share his glory and everlasting happiness" (161).

Summarizing, we might say: in the Old Testament, all things pointed to Christ, evolved toward Him and were fulfilled in Him. In the New Dispensation, however, Christ is our Head, who offered the sacrifice of His daily life until the very Cross, not only for our benefit but also in our stead. In these Messianic times, therefore, God's plan for mankind is not that of evolution toward a goal already achieved in our Head. Our aim in life as Christians is to become "a worthy altar on which the various phases of the Sacrifice offered by the High Priest as it were come to life again" (*Mediator Dei, 152*).

PART FOUR

I. MARY, MODEL OF OUR WORSHIP

Devotion to Mary is an essential and treasured part of our faith. We are grateful to God that our separated brethren of the Eastern Orthodox Churches share this devotion with us and that it is a major bond of union with them. And we lament the fact that for many of our separated brethren of the Protestant Churches our devotion to Mary has become, both doctrinally but perhaps even more psychologically, a rock of stumbling. Perhaps all Catholics have had the experience, in talking with a sincere and well-instructed Protestant about matters of religion, that before long he will inevitably bring up the question of Mariology: that he is honestly perturbed by what he considers the exaggerated role which Mary plays in Catholic doctrine and devotional life—to the neglect (he is convinced) of the unique mediatorial and redemptive role of Christ, the one Mediator between God and Man.

This rock of stumbling has loomed large on the path to reunion ever since the Protestant Reformation. As René Laurentin, one of the best modern historians of Mariology, has pointed out, the Protestantism of the sixteenth century rejected the developments of the intervening centuries and accepted only the

Mariology of the time of the Council of Ephesus in 431, limiting it to the three fundamentals: the sanctity and virginity of Mary, and her motherhood of God; and sometimes it would eliminate even these.

It is not for us to apportion blame, subjective personal blame, for this tragic loss of Christian heritage. But we can and should, in sorrow and humble regret, be aware of the historical context in which this grievous loss occurred.

For, the same historian informs us, Mariology, especially in its popular devotional forms, was at its lowest ebb just when the Protestant crisis arose. "The favorite Marian author just then was Bernardino dei Busti, whose *Mariale,* first published in 1496, went through numerous editions. It is an indication of the decadence of the period that it should have esteemed so highly a work such as this, for, though it certainly contains some excellent ideas, these are too often drowned in a welter of exaggerations and inconsistencies."

And we must further admit, again with humble regret, that some of these exaggerations and inconsistencies, especially in expressions of Marian piety which are visible because publicly advertised to the outside world, continue to stir apprehension in the minds and hearts of even the well disposed among our Protestant friends. Rome itself has in our day more than once warned against excesses in devotion to Mary. True, the same documents have warned also against the opposite danger of deficiencies. But the fact that our Catholic diocesan press headlined the warning against excesses indicates probably that this part of the document seemed, at least to the editors, more immediately applicable to our own conditions.

Very much to the point is a letter written at the request of Pope Pius XII to a national congress of Catholic clergy at Vicenza, Italy, in 1954, by the then Monsignor Montini, pro-Secretary of State:

"There is no need to speak about the precious fruits that would come to each and all within the Church if this powerful impulse of love for Mary, which gives to our troubled times its brightest note of confidence, were formed and disciplined according to the spirit of liturgical worship. Our relations to the Virgin, far from exhausting themselves in superficial sentimentality or in anxious and self-interested pleading for help in moments of need, would thereby acquire that character of maturity and depth so necessary for perseverance and fruitfulness in the spiritual life."

This statement is obviously an echo of the encyclical on the liturgy, *Mediator Dei,* which while reminding us in forceful terms that the liturgy is not the whole of Catholic piety, insists that it is the exemplar, the yardstick by which all forms of private devotion must be measured.

Very briefly, therefore, let us sketch the chief lessons which the liturgy offers us in guiding our devotion to the Blessed Virgin.

1) The first lesson: Mary must occupy a prominent role in our piety. A mere superficial glance at the Missal suffices to convince us of this. There are eighteen universal liturgical feasts of Mary, fifteen of which have their own Mass propers. Further, there is a common of the Blessed Virgin and five votive Masses for Saturdays according to the seasons. (It might be remembered, too, that the simplification of the calendar and rubrics of September, 1955, and of August, 1960, left an increased number of times for this Saturday Mass in honor of the Blessed Virgin to be celebrated.) There are also a number of other feasts in the year which are observed primarily because of a relation to Mary: e.g., St. Gabriel, St. Joachim and St. Anne.

Most significant of all, Mary is prominently mentioned no less than five times in the ordinary of every Mass—and, whether by happy coincidence or by design, such mention occurs in each of the parts of the Mass: foremass, offertory, canon, and communion. She accompanies us all the way, on this Way which is of the essence of our life.

2) The second lesson of the liturgy: the feasts of Mary are echoes, images of the redemptive feasts of our Lord.

Christ	*Mary*
Conception-Annunciation	Immaculate Conception
Birth	Birthday of Mary
Holy Name	Name of Mary
Presentation of Christ in the Temple	Presentation
Passion	Sorrows of Mary

Resurrection	Assumption
Kingship	Queenship
Sacred Heart	Immaculate Heart of Mary

History, moreover, informs us that the first feast of Mary in the West was what, until the new calendar of 1960, was called the feast of Circumcision, but which in various prayers and especially in its antiphons always revealed that it was originally a Mary-feast. That is to say, the octave day of Christmas was the feast of Mary. For she is the echo, the image of Christ: His associate in the mysteries of redemption—or, as the earliest Fathers, beginning with Justin, Irenaeus, Tertullian, etc., phrased it: Mary is the Second Eve, the associate of Christ, our Second Adam.

3) The third lesson of the liturgy concerns the content of Mary's imaging of Christ. The Mass liturgy usually contains its most important didactic lesson in the gospel. Now the gospel of the common of the Blessed Virgin Mary is the one most frequently used for her feasts. Luke in this gospel tells us that on one occasion, while Christ was preaching, a woman in the crowd raised her voice and said: "Blessed is the womb that bore thee and the breasts that gave thee suck." Jesus answered: *"Yea rather,* blessed are they who hear the word of God and keep it."

At first hearing this account may almost shock us. Christ seems almost to brush aside the praise of His mother which this woman in the crowd had uttered.

And the mystery apparently becomes more insoluble when we recall a similar incident related in Matthew and Mark. These evangelists report that while Jesus was speaking to the crowds, His mother and His brethren were standing outside seeking to speak to Him. Someone told Jesus: "Behold thy mother and thy brethren are standing outside seeking thee." Now one would expect a loving Son in such circumstances to hurry outside to greet and welcome His mother. "But," the evangelist continues, "Jesus answered and said to him who told him: Who is my mother and who are my brethren? And stretching forth his hand toward his disciples, he said: Behold my mother and my brethren. For whosoever does the will of my Father in heaven, he is my brother and sister and mother."

St. Augustine, commenting on the incident in a homily which the Church has selected for her readings in the breviary, solves the difficulty, if such it be for us. He states emphatically that Mary's greatness and her holiness do not consist primarily in the fact that she was physically the mother of Jesus. Rather, Mary is all holy, Mary is blessed and full of grace because she was most like Christ in mind and will. Or, as other early Fathers of the Church like to phrase it: Mary conceived and was Christ's mother spiritually (*mente*) even before she conceived and was His mother bodily. And Père Prat agrees that such is the traditional teaching.

This should, I am convinced, be a great and consoling doctrine for us. If we think almost exclusively of the merely physical maternity of Mary as the reason and source of her holiness, we by that fact make her as it were remote from us. She is, in that case, holy because of something entirely and absolutely unattainable by us. We can, then, hardly experience in its full impact the urgency of imitating her—precisely because her holiness seems of such an entirely different order. Surely, blessed is the womb that bore Christ and the breasts that gave Him suck. But even more so, blessed is she because she heard the word of God so eagerly and kept it so perfectly. It is the same St. Luke, indeed, who earlier in his Gospel twice records how Mary heard the word of God—and pondered it in her heart.

Christ's whole life of sacrifice can be summed up in His own words: "Not my will but thine be done." Mary was the worthy mother of such a son, utterly one with Him, because she could summarize her own life and will in the words: "Be it done unto me according to Thy word." Christ described His task on earth: "I came not to be ministered unto but to minister." Mary anticipated His declaration when she answered the angel of the annunciation: "Behold the handmaid of the Lord."

And that is why we rejoice to celebrate Mary's feasts by celebrating the holy sacrifice of Mass, as we say, in her honor. We pay her homage; we promise to imitate our mother. And she leads us into the sacrifice of her divine Son; she leads us, by encouraging us, by reminding us how, like herself, we can and must be united to the sacrificial will of Christ, in which is all our holiness. She leads us: for do we not pray in every Mass:

"*communicantes*—sharing in the sentiments of the Blessed Virgin . . . we offer." As at that other banquet which foreshadowed the Eucharist, at Cana, so here also she exhorts us: "Do whatever He tells you."

There is a common saying: Like mother like son. In this case, we should rather say: Like Son like Mother. There are two great *Ecce's* in sacred Scripture: *Ecce Agnus Dei*, and *Ecce ancilla Domini*.

God is holy. He alone is holy. *Tu solus sanctus*. And all human holiness is a sharing in the holiness of God. All human holiness means conformity of the human mind and heart to the mind and will of God. That is true also of the humanity of Christ; His first and ultimate concern was the glory of the Father. And that is why Mary is the first among all the saints and, after Christ, as the image of Christ, also their model—because she was, in faith and charity, so completely *God-centered*.

It is again St. Luke who, quoting the archangel and St. Elizabeth, hails Mary, "Blessed among women and blessed is the fruit of thy womb"—but then adds: "Beata quia *credidisti*." Blessed is she because she has believed—because she has *consented* wholly to God.

Mary's God-centeredness, her total willingness to conform in all things to the designs of God—if this is the basic lesson of Scripture and the liturgy concerning Mary as our model and spiritual Mother, has it been equally basic in motivating our devotion to Mary? Perhaps the answer is not entirely reassuring. We have stressed, perhaps all too selfishly and onesidedly, her role as intercessor, as dispenser of graces. Have we honored her equally for the reason that God honored her—even to the extent of making her the mother of His Son—*quia credidisti*? We have regarded anthropocentrically her who above all others is theocentric.

And by neglecting this more important reason for venerating Mary, by concentrating on the more self-interested aspect of receiving benefits through her help, have we perhaps contributed unwittingly to render much more difficult a true understanding of Mary's role on the part of our Protestant brethren? Have we thereby indeed impoverished our own understanding of the great prerogatives of Mary, which we have too much isolated instead of seeing them in perspective?

I shall merely point out, very summarily, how this basic dimension of Mary's God-centeredness throws wonderful light on some of these prerogatives and the honors that the Church has traditionally paid to Mary.

Immaculate Conception. This does not mean just sinlessness. But for the first time now, since the fall of man, here was a human being without unruly concupiscence, without being distracted by the things of this world from fulfilling undividedly the purpose of God in creating man: to give Him glory. Mary is the diamond without flaw that reflects without distortion the light of God. No wonder that Péguy could exclaim that with the conception of Mary a completely new chapter was begun in the history of mankind.

Virginity. Why has the Church from the very outset been so jealous in defending the ever-virginity of Mary? Not because she disparages marriage—but because virginity, Christian virginity, means, not just abstention from marital rights but something gloriously positive: total and immediate personal dedication in love to the person of the beloved, God Himself.

The Divine Maternity. Here belong all those insights of the Fathers who speak of Mary conceiving in her heart, in her totally God-dedicated and consenting will, before she conceived bodily in her womb. The physical divine motherhood can in a very true sense be called the fruit, the consequence, of Mary's *fiat,* her spiritual motherhood.

The Presentation of Mary in the Temple. This, one of the earliest feasts of Mary in the East, and still regarded by many of our Eastern brethren as one of the chief mysteries of the year, did not depend on historical evidence. Whether Mary literally dedicated herself to God at the age of three in the Temple was and is secondary to the symbolic significance of the feast: that Mary from her infancy thirsted to serve God most fully.

The Assumption. Mary, the first of the redeemed, is the first also who with *body* and soul has achieved the goal of redemption: the eternal worship of God. She is Queen of Heaven, Queen of the Angels who surround the throne of God, singing their never ceasing *Sanctus.* Mary on earth was not, judging from scriptural evidence, loquacious. But she did, on one occasion, express her whole life's essence in the eloquent *Magnificat*: my soul magnifies the Lord. Her assumption made that canticle eternal. (Is it a permissible fancy to think of her teaching both words and melodies to the heavenly choir? After all, St. Augustine in a sermon which the Church has enshrined in her breviary lessons for September 8 does call her our *tympanistria*—the tymbral-shaking leader of the dancing chorus [cf. Ex. 15:20]. And I submit that this is certainly as meaningful and edifying as presenting her as Madonna of the goldfinch.)

Nor need we fear that by honoring her as our model of worship, by stressing her God-centeredness, we are (to put it crudely) shortchanging ourselves—that she will somehow be less concerned with us. Rather, it is our great consolation to know that precisely the measure of her concern for God is the measure of her love for us. Here again, Scripture enlightens us, to our spiritual comfort—*and* to stir us to emulation in apostolic effort.

Immediately after narrating Mary's God-centered *Fiat*, Luke adds: "And Mary arose *in haste*" and went into the hill country, to be of service to her cousin Elizabeth. And it was at the other great climactic moment of her union with God's will, at the foot of the cross, that Christ, not as it were even allowing Mary the luxury of grief, or rather of sole concentration on Himself, asked her henceforth to serve all mankind: "Behold thy son."

Now in the beatific vision Mary loves us for the identical, consciously accepted reasons that God loves us, and in that absorbing vision she knows our needs. Because she has her face turned wholly toward God, she sees us more clearly. No, we do not have to fear that Mary's God-centeredness will make her less our mother. But only by making her the model of our worship, by freely and more wholeheartedly imitating her God-centeredness, can we hope to become her worthy sons.

II. THE HIGH PRIESTHOOD OF THE BISHOP

The evangelist St. John, in one of his visions recorded in the book of Apocalypse, speaks in mysterious words of "the Lamb who has been slain from the foundation of the world" (13:8). The Lamb, of course, is the High Priest and Victim, Jesus, who is enthroned for all eternity on the heavenly altar. In other words, from the beginning of the human race to its final glorification, from the first book of the Bible, Genesis, to the last book, the Apocalypse, the Priest and Victim Christ is central: from beginning to end, and in every age of time in between.

St. John, by speaking of the Lamb slain from the foundation of the world, wishes to remind us that God at no time since the sin of our first parents had totally rejected or deserted the fallen human race. Always and everywhere, according to the law that He Himself had written into the hearts of men, there was sacrifice and priesthood. And however imperfect, however distorted and even corrupt, so long as there was good will, such sacrifice and priesthood was a foreshadowing of the perfect sacrifice and priesthood of the Lamb of God.

Such, certainly, is the lesson the Church herself teaches us, when in the canon of the Mass she prays that God be pleased to accept this sacrifice of the High Priest Christ as He was pleased to accept the sacrifices of Abel (which we can truly say was from the foundation of the world), of Abraham (the father of *all* the faithful, both Jew and Gentile), and of Melchisedech (the Gentile high priest). At all times God was the Lord to be adored and to be placated for sin. At all times, from the foundation of the world, there was some form of priesthood and sacrifice.

But when God decided to establish His own chosen people, to prepare more immediately for the coming of the true High Priest, He established also a special priesthood, and legislated in great detail how that priesthood was to function, and what

Liturgical Week 1951, Dubuque, Iowa.

sacrifices it was to offer. The entire book of Leviticus and a large part of Numbers is devoted to that legislation. The Jews were to be His chosen people, because they were to worship Him more worthily. The Jews were the people of God because they were a people whose whole life and history centered in priesthood and sacrifice. Hence, when God, through Moses, established His covenant with them, He said: "You shall be to me a *priestly* kingdom, and a holy nation" (Ex. 19:6).

So much, most of us will well remember from our reading of the Old Testament. But there is another aspect of the story which, I think, is of the utmost importance in order to understand aright the preparatory priesthood of the Old Testament and the fulfillment of that priesthood in the New. I mean the *presence* of God among His priestly people. It is this presence of God among His chosen race which is *the* distinguishing characteristic of the Old Covenant. The Jews now had priests and sacrifice. They could worship God in a manner that He Himself had determined. But the great, the marvelous, the unheard-of result was His dwelling in their midst. That God "whom no man has seen at any time," that God, the Creator of heaven and earth, the God of hosts whom no man can "see and live" (Ex. 33:20), that same terrible and great God now mercifully showed His presence among them by visible, unmistakable signs.

When He entered upon His covenant with His priestly kingdom, all Mount Sinai was on smoke: because the Lord was come down upon it in fire, and "the smoke arose from it as out of a furnace; and all the mount was terrible" (Ex. 19:18). When God gave to Moses the tables of the commandments, "a cloud covered the mount. And the glory of the Lord dwelt upon Sinai. . . . And the sight of the glory of the Lord was like a burning fire upon the top of the mount, in the eyes of the children of Israel" (Ex. 24:15–17).

But most especially was this presence of God manifested often and mightily on occasions of priestly worship. When God gave directions for the making of the tabernacle, He spoke to Moses, saying: "And they shall make me a sanctuary and I will dwell in the midst of them" (Ex. 25:8). And after this tabernacle of the covenant had been set up and anointed, God filled it with His majesty in visible form: "The cloud of the Lord hung over the tabernacle by day, and a fire by night . . . and the glory of the Lord filled it" (Ex. 40:36, 32). Again, God commanded Moses to choose seventy men of the ancients of Israel, to help him rule the people: "And thou shalt bring them to the door of the tabernacle of the covenant. . . . And the Lord came down in a cloud . . . taking of the spirit that was in Moses, and giving to the seventy men" (Num. 11:16, 25). (How priestly this occasion was, by the way, can be seen from the fact that it is cited in the ordination to holy orders, by which the bishop similarly chooses men to assist him in his work as high priest).

Above all, however, this visible presence of God among His people is centered in the Temple of sacrifice. At its dedication by Solomon, "the majesty of the Lord filled the house. Neither could the priests enter into the temple of the Lord, because the majesty of the Lord filled the temple of the Lord. And all the children of Israel saw . . . the glory of the Lord upon the house, and falling down, . . . they adored and praised the Lord" (II Par. 7:1–3). Jerusalem was the *Holy* City, because it was the city that God Himself had chosen as His own capital city, His residential city; the Temple was His residential palace, and the ark of the covenant in the Temple was His throne. Here He dwelt, seated on the outspread wings of the cherubim.

Priest and sacrifice in the Old Law, therefore, entailed the mysterious but real presence of God among His holy people. If we can speak of a "glad tidings" in the Old Testament, this was certainly it. The psalms are full of it. "Glorious things are said of thee, O city of God" (Ps. 86:3). "In Judea God is known; His name is great in Israel: for His place is in peace (i.e., in Jerusalem) and His abode in Zion" (Ps. 75:1–2). That is why the annual pilgrimage to the Temple was such a joyous event: "I rejoiced in the things that were said to me: we shall go up into the house of the Lord" (Ps. 121:1; cf. all the Gradual Psalms). The Temple was truly the "house of the Lord," not only dedicated to Him, but taken possession of by Him as His own dwelling. Here, in the midst of His people, He ruled them, and accepted the worshipful homage of their priests and their sacrifices. And therefore the pious Jews prayed: "If I shall forget thee, O Jerusalem, let my right hand be forgotten; let my tongue cleave to my jaws, if I do not remember thee, if I make not Jerusalem the beginning of my joy."

Now all of this may seem like an unnecessarily lengthy introduction. But its importance should, I think, be obvious. Priesthood and sacrificial worship in the Old Testament brought with them a certain presence of God among His people. It was a real presence, but also a presence shrouded in mystery. It was a presence *in a cloud*. The glory of God shone, but it shone through a cloud; it was not yet fully revealed.

When the fullness of time was come, however, when the priesthood of the Old Testament was fulfilled in the priesthood of Christ, John could cry out: "We *have seen* His glory, the glory of the only-begotten of the Father" (John 1:14). If the presence of God among His priestly people of the Old Testament was a wonderful, unheard-of thing, His presence now is immeasurably more so! For now He is present, not merely as a God to be placated by His human priests: such worship would always be pitifully, infinitely, inadequate. Now He is *Emmanuel,* "God with us!" "The goodness and kindness of God our Savior has appeared" (Tit. 3:4), the Christmas liturgy exults. He has come over, as it were, entirely on our side. He has become "one of us," our elder brother. By becoming man, the Son of God became our High Priest, giving us power, in our turn, to become sons of God.

Of this priesthood of Christ I have treated somewhat in a previous chapter. I would merely like to stress that this new, this perfect priesthood in the New Testament means the presence of God among men: such a new and marvelous presence that it effects our life-union with God. It is not merely the presence of a gracious God among His worshipping servants: it is the grace-conferring presence of a brother who shares His divine life with His brethren.

We can still feel the thrill of wonder in St. John's description of that presence of which he had been witness: "I write of what was from the beginning, *what we have heard, what we have seen* with our eyes, what we have looked upon *and our hands have handled:* of the Word of Life. And the Life was made known and we have seen, and now testify and announce to you, the Life Eternal which was with the Father, and has appeared to us. What we have seen and have heard we announce to you, in order that you also may have fellowship with us, and that our fellowship may be with the Father, and with His Son Jesus Christ. And these things we write to you that you may rejoice, and our joy may be full" (I John 1:1–4). Or, as the same John says in the beginning of his Gospel: "The Word was made flesh, *and dwelt among us. And we saw His glory* . . . full of grace and truth. . . . And of His fullness we have all received" (John 1:14–16).

Such, therefore, is the glad tidings of the New Covenant: the *presence,* the epiphany, among us of God become man, of God become a *priest,* in order to grant us union of life with Himself and the Father.

And if we read the New Testament carefully, we shall notice that it is a chief function of the apostles to bear witness to that presence of Christ the Priest, and of the saving acts of priesthood that He had performed in their midst. In fact, the word "witness" is a key word in the early story of the Church. Thus Christ, instructing the apostles to go out and continue His own priestly work, promised them: "But you shall receive power when the Holy Spirit comes upon you, and you shall be witnesses for me in Jerusalem and in all Judea and Samaria and even to the very ends of the earth" (Acts 1:8). At the Last Supper, after He had consecrated them priests, He had similarly promised: "When the Advocate has come, the Spirit of truth . . . He will bear witness concerning me. And you also bear witness, because from the beginning you are with me" (John 15:26 f.). Thus when the apostles gathered together to choose a successor to the apostolic office left vacant by the traitor Judas, they were concerned to select one "who had been in our company all the time that the Lord Jesus moved among us—of these one must become a witness with us of his resurrection" (Acts 1:21–22). Again, when the Lord appeared to Saul on the road to Damascus, He said: "I am Jesus whom thou art persecuting. But rise and stand upon thy feet: for I have appeared to thee for this purpose, to appoint thee to be a minister and a witness to what thou hast seen" (Acts 26:16). The priestly work of the apostles is, therefore, a bearing witness to the world of the presence of Christ the Priest among men.

But it is yet more. Far more. Not only are the apostles to *bear* witness to Christ the Priest. Rather, Christ's priestly presence among men is perpetuated in their persons. They are personalized witnesses. In their priestly work, they are nothing less than the *visible sign* of His own high priestly presence and activity. For Christ had said: "He who receives you, receives me" (Mt. 10:40). And again: "He who hears you, hears me" (Luke 10:16). He could just as well have said: "He who sees you sees Me"—as He had said of Himself: "He who sees Me, sees the Father." And yet again: "As the Father has sent me, so I also send you" (John 20:21). And lest there be any misunderstanding, He in a most solemn manner declared when giving them their priestly commission: "All power in heaven and on earth is given to me. Go, therefore, and make disciples of all nations, baptizing them in the name of the Father and of the Son and of the Holy Spirit . . . and behold, *I am with you all days* even to the consummation of the world" (Mt. 28:19–20).

"I am with you." Christ is present with the apostles, and thus with their successors, the bishops of the Church, for all time, acting in and through them. They are visible symbols of His saving presence among us. *The New Testament is not less than the Old.* In the persons of our bishops, we have a visible guarantee of the more wonderful high priestly presence of God among His people. And therefore the term "high priest," reserved in the New Testament to Christ alone, is now fittingly applied by the Church to each of her bishops. *Ecce sacerdos magnus*—"Behold the high priest." With these words the Church officially greets her bishops. In every bishop is realized anew what was prophesied of old and fulfilled perfectly in Christ: "Behold the high priest . . . The Lord took an oath that he should be the father of his chosen people. The Lord gave Him the blessing which should extend to all nations, renewing the covenant in his person. . . . The Lord made Him great in the sight of kings . . . He made a covenant with Him forever, entrusting him with the great office of the priesthood, and enriching him with high honor. He was to serve the Lord as his priest, privileged to act in his name and to offer incense to him, acceptable in its fragrance" (Ecclus. 44:16–45:20; used as a lesson in the Mass of a confessor bishop). The Church's prayer asks that the people may through his visit experience the advent of God Himself. Or, as Pope Pius XII summarized the matter in his encyclical on the Mystical Body: "It is through them (the bishops) commissioned by the divine Redeemer Himself, that Christ's apostolate as teacher, king, priest, is to endure" (par. 21, America Press edition). "Individual Christian communities . . . are ruled by *Jesus Christ*, through the voice of their own respective bishops" (Ibid., par. 52).

The most eminent way, however, in which the bishop is the living symbol of the High Priest Christ lies in his offering the holy sacrifice. This is evident from the fact that the apostles were ordained high priests, not when Christ sent them out to preach, nor when He told them, "Whatsoever you shall bind," etc. They became high priests when at the Last Supper He told them: "Do *this* in memory of me." The bishop is not then, first of all, one who has jurisdiction over a diocese. A bishop is he who has been commissioned by Christ to offer the Holy Eucharist in His name and person.

For that reason the first text of the consecration of a bishop which has come down to us (in the *Apostolic Tradition*, written by St. Hippolytus about the year 215), mentions his office of high priestly, Eucharistic worship first of all: "Pour down the power of Thy sovereign Spirit, with which Thou didst, by Thy beloved Son Jesus Christ, give grace to Thy holy apostles who founded Thy Church . . . Give unto Thy servant here present, chosen by Thee for the episcopate, that he may feed Thy flock, and serve Thee as a high priest without reproach, rendering Thee worship . . . and to offer Thee the gifts of Thy holy Church." Therefore it is, too, that to our own day, the first high priestly function the newly consecrated bishop performs is to offer the holy sacrifice. St. Thomas says simply: "Holy orders is instituted primarily for the sake of the sacrament of the Holy Eucharist; all the other purposes (e.g. ruling, teaching) are secondary" (*Summa Theol.* III, Suppl. q. 37, a. 2, ad 3). The bishop is never so much a bishop, a high priest of Christ, as when, surrounded by his people, he offers the Eucharist for them and in their name and, as shepherd, feeds his flock. That is his greatest privilege and honor, his primary task.

The bishop is master of the Eucharist in his diocese. For does not the Apocalypse describe the *throne* of the Lamb (i.e., His ruling power) as the *altar of sacrifice?* Just as the Cross was altar first, and then throne, the wood from which Christ reigns. And hence St. Paul could say: "He humbled himself, becoming obedient unto death, even the death of the cross. *Therefore* God also has *exalted* Him and has bestowed upon Him the name that is above every name, so that at the name of Jesus every knee should bend of those in heaven, on earth, and under the earth" (Phil. 2:6–10).

It is by celebrating the Eucharist as high priest of his flock that the bishop bears most eloquent and potent *witness* to the presence of Christ the High Priest: "Do this in remembrance of Me. For as often as you shall eat this bread and drink this cup, you *proclaim* the death of the Lord, until He comes" (I Cor. 11:25 f.). His glory is to be "servant of Christ, and *minister of the mysteries of God*" (I Cor. 4:1). And the sum and center of these mysteries is the *Mysterium Fidei,* the Mystery of the Altar.

Those who have assisted at the episcopal consecration of a bishop will remember vividly, therefore, how the rite of consecration underscores this identity between the bishop and Christ the High Priest. The essential words of consecration pray God to "complete in *thy priest the highest fullness* of thy ministry" (*ministerii*: the ancient, traditional word used here was *mysterii*). And then there is the wonderful, ancient rite, as old certainly as the fourth century, in which the open gospel book is held over his head. We have, unfortunately, almost forgotten its real meaning. The gospel book is a symbol of Christ. Holding it open, above the new bishop's head, is a vivid sign of Christ's *presence and power* descending upon and filling the person of the bishop. (Cf. Pseudo-Denys's explanation in his *De Ecclesiastica Hierarchia*). The bishop now, in the fullest possible sense of the word, is a Christ-bearer. With the eyes of faith we must see Christ, our High Priest and giver of spiritual life, in the person of our bishop. Pius XII, in his encyclical on the Mystical Body accordingly exhorts us: "We must accustom ourselves to see Christ in the Church. It is Christ who lives in the Church, who teaches and governs and sanctifies through her. It is Christ, too, who manifests Himself differently in different members of His society. Once the faithful try to live in this spirit of conscious faith, they will . . . pay due honor and reverence to the superior members of this Mystical Body" (par. 110).

That means, in a concrete way, that one of the great objectives of the liturgical movement must be to develop among our priests and faithful a closer bond of love and reverence between themselves and their bishop, their high priest. We must again come to realize what it means that our bishop is our spiritual father, the dispenser of divine life. Above all, we must feel closely bound to him in the sacrifice of the Eucharistic sacrifice in his diocese. When he ordains priests, he ordains them as his collaborators: *cooperatores ordinis nostri*, collaborators of our order, he calls them. And true to his idea, the newly ordained priests immediately co-offer the one Sacrifice of which he, the bishop, is *the* celebrant. And so it will be throughout their priestly life in their parishes. Every Mass, in every parish, is so to speak *an extension* of the Eucharistic Sacrifice celebrated by your high priest, the bishop. In every Mass you are united to your spiritual father, your bishop; you in turn are sharing in the sacrifice that *he* offers.[1] That was made very clear in ancient times in Rome itself. The bishop, i.e., the pope, sent a part

[1] I am aware that this interpretation of the high priesthood of the bishop primarily in terms of his role as celebrant *per eminentiam* of the Eucharistic Sacrifice, which power he communicates and delegates as it were to his priests, his Eucharistic *cooperatores*, though it corresponds to his premises, cannot cite St. Thomas as a supporter. But (besides the reasons given) it seems to me to do fuller justice to the primarily sacrificial (Eucharistic) connotation of the "priesthood" of the New Testament, to the history of the development of parishes, and to so much of earlier tradition. Thus St. Ignatius Martyr, writing to the Smyrnaeans, says: "Let no one do any of the things appertaining to the Church without the bishop. Let that be considered a valid Eucharist which is celebrated by the bishop, or *by one whom he appoints*. Wherever the bishop appears let the congregation be present; just as wherever Jesus Christ is, there is the Catholic Church" (VIII, 1, 2). The argument from tradition was most recently presented, with considerable persuasiveness, by the dogma professor Jean Colson in *Nouvelle Revue Théologique* (December, 1951), 1049–59.

of the consecrated bread of his Mass to each of the parishes of the city, where it was placed in the sacred chalice before Communion time. There could hardly have been a more eloquent reminder that the parish Mass is really an extension of the bishop's Mass, and that the bishop himself is, as it were, administering Holy Communion to his flock through the hands of his "collaborators," his priests.

The same lesson is moreover taught us by the crucifix on the main altar of our parish church. The cross is a solemn sign of Christ's high priestly sacrifice. Accordingly, for centuries the cross was a sign of the high priesthood, which only the bishop had a right to (much in the same way as a pectoral cross, nowadays, is reserved to prelates).

Similarly the cross was carried in procession only when the bishop was celebrant, and then placed in front of the altar while Mass was being offered. That is the origin of our crucifix on the altar. It is therefore an historical and constant reminder of our union with our high priests, our bishop, by means of the Eucharistic Sacrifice. (And if we need still other reminders of this same fact, we need but recall that it is the bishop, as high priest of the Eucharist, who consecrates altars and chalices.)

The spiritual bond between all members of the diocese and their high priest, the bishop, is, of course, evident also in other sacraments. He it is who consecrates the sacred oils which are used in baptism, confirmation and extreme unction. It is the bishop who gives jurisdiction to his representatives, his priests, to administer penance and to assist at weddings. All these sacraments, accordingly, deepen our union with our great spiritual father. The bishop, moreover, is obliged personally to preach the word of God to his flock (Can. 1327, par. 1), so that, echoing St. Paul, he too can say of all his flock: "In the gospel I have begotten you" (I Cor. 4:14). With great reverence, therefore, we should listen to his pastoral letters, for it is Christ through our bishop who is addressing us.

So real are these spiritual relations between the bishop and his entire diocese, that tradition, from the first century, has spoken of him as "wedded" to his diocese, as Christ is wedded to His bride, the Church. St. Thomas says, with his usual incisiveness: "A bishop is in a special manner called the bride-groom of the Church, even as Christ is" (*Summa Theol.*, III, Suppl., q. 40, a. 4, ad 3). That, as you know, is the meaning of his episcopal ring. It is a wedding ring, for by his consecration he has become the head, the father, of a spiritual family. When he receives the ring, therefore, he is told: "Receive this ring, the seal of *fidelity*, so that you may preserve spotless, with un-tainted fidelity, the bride of Christ which is the Church." And Pope Innocent III did not hesitate to comment that the bonds of spiritual marriage between a bishop and his flock are closer and more binding than the bonds of carnal marriage (*Inter corporalia*, 2, X, *de translatione episcopi*). Because the bishop is wedded to his diocese, there can only be one bishop truly head of a diocese, and that for life. And when he dies, the diocese is referred to in official, traditional, language as being widowed (*viduata*).

The exalted position of the bishop as high priest and living symbol of the presence of Christ in our midst demands, too, that his church, the cathedral parish, occupy a very special posi-tion in the esteem and affection of all his people. It is perhaps unfortunate that in our own time the cathedral, in most dioceses, is hardly much more than a parish church in which the bishop happens to pontificate on more important occasions. As a matter of fact, however, the cathedral church is the *mother* church of the diocese. It represents the *whole* diocese. We might call it *the* parish church to which all members of the diocese first of all belong, and of which their own parish churches are only an extension or irradiation.

For it is the church of which their high priestly spiritual father is the real pastor. All should feel at home in it. All should feel an obligation towards it. All should take part in celebrating the annual feast of its dedication. And when opportunity offers they should visit their mother church, and assist at services there. It might not be a bad idea at all, for a parish, or for families, to make a pilgrimage to their cathedral church. It is certainly more sacred and important than any shrine: for it is their spiritual home, the center and hearth from which their spiritual life originates. Need it be added that those who are, more directly, members of the cathedral parish, should appreciate their spiritual privilege? They should regard themselves as *representative* of all the people of the diocese, and should feel a corresponding obligation to represent them worthily, with greater devotion, especially at Holy Mass—and at vespers or compline, which, if anywhere, certainly deserve to be celebrated in the Mother Church, the visible symbol of the *Ecclesia orans*, of the Church at prayer.

As to the priesthood as exercised by the parish priest, it is only in the light of the fullness of high priestly power that this collaboratory ministry can be truly understood. For it is priests' glory to be sharers in the great mystery and in the holiness of their high priest. As Anger phrases it: "Priests are not the center of unity as is the bishop. They have only those powers conferred upon them by the bishop" (Anger-Burke, *Doctrine of the Mystical Body*, p. 185).

True, the individual Catholic and the Christian community *experience* the Church directly and immediately in their own parishes. The famous German scholar, Romano Guardini, has characterized our age as the age in which the "Church is coming to life in the hearts of men." And he spoke truly. This is the age of the Mystical Body. But if the Mystical Body is to be more than a nice abstraction, it must be realized and experienced first of all in the community of the parish, of which the pastor is the living Christ. Pius XI, speaking to the pastors of Rome (Feb. 11, 1929) stated emphatically: "The parish is a family, whose home is the parish church, and whose hearth is the altar . . . The parish church and altar must permeate the entire life of the parishioners." And it is no doubt symbolically providential, that in this age of the mystical body, Pius X, the parish priest in the chair of Peter, was raised to the dignity of the altars.

The parish is indeed, as Pius XI also stated, "the primary cell of the spiritual life of the entire family of the Church" (*Pio XI e l'Azione Cattolica*, Rome, 1930, p. 83). But the fullness of that life can be lived only by the spiritual family which is the diocese. The great St. Cyprian summarizes it in ringing words: "This is the Church: the people united to the bishop, the

flock faithful to their shepherd. . . . The bishop is in the
Church, and the Church is in the bishop. If anyone be not
with the bishop, he is not in the Church" (*Ep.* 69, n. 8:
PL IV, 406).

III. REFLECTIONS ON EUCHARISTIC FAST

St. Pius X's decree concerning frequent and even daily Communion was without doubt one of the great milestones in the
history of Christian spirituality. Yet we know that the hopes he
cherished were not so universally realized as he would have
wished. It always takes time, of course, for people to readjust
themselves to new ideas. But there is also another reason why
the ideal of frequent Communion was not more widely carried
into effect. Pastoral experience over the years discovered that a
chief hindrance existed in the traditional rules of the Eucharistic
fast. And with our rapidly developing industrial civilization, and
the corresponding changes in daily living, this obstacle had become all the more formidable. Night has been turned into day:
and I am not referring merely to night shifts of labor, but also
to the sport-shirt shift whose day begins after supper. In a word,
for an increasingly large number of people, Pope Pius X's ideal
of frequent and even daily Communion became, practically
speaking, impossible.

We owe therefore a very great debt of gratitude to Pius XII,
who, forty-eight years after Pius X's decree on frequent Communion, issued the apostolic constitution *Christus Dominus.*
In it, by changing the rules of the Eucharistic fast, he removed
the chief obstacles to the realization of Pius X's hopes.

Pius XII enumerates eight reasons which had made frequent
Communion difficult. All eight of them have to do with the
Eucharistic fast, whether of priests or people. "Wherefore," he
sums up, "that We may meet these grave inconveniences and

difficulties, We have deemed it necessary to lay down the discipline of the Eucharistic fast, by mitigating it in such a way that, in the greatest manner possible, all, in view of the peculiar circumstances of time, place and the faithful, may be able to fulfill this law more easily. We by this decree trust that We may be able to . . . stir up all to partake at the Table of the Angels."

The traditional fast, which in its origin was meant to increase Eucharistic piety, and dispose the faithful to receive the greatest possible benefits from the Eucharist, had, because of altered circumstances, come to decrease Eucharistic piety by preventing the very reception of the Body and Blood of Christ. The Eucharistic fast was like a hedge around the garden of Eucharistic piety: a good, strong hedge, to allow the fair garden within to grow and thrive; but in the course of time, it became instead a hedge keeping out of the garden itself those who had a right and need to enter.

And yet the solution of the problem is not to tear down the hedge; for the hedge does serve a most useful purpose. But openings are to be cleared through the hedge, gates and doors that invite entry, and yet exclude undesirables and those unworthy.

In other words, the principle of the Eucharistic fast in itself is far too precious an inheritance, far too necessary a help to Eucharistic piety, to be rejected, or even criticized. Changes, modifications, yes; but not abolition.

That certainly was the mind of Pope Pius XII. I would like to urge a reading not only of the new rules of fasting, but of the entire apostolic constitution. It is very clear that the Pope insists on the spiritual necessity of a Eucharistic fast, in our time as much as in all previous centuries. After briefly sketching the history of the Eucharistic fast, he proceeds to give four major reasons why such a fast is and always has been important. And in conclusion he again insists: "It has pleased Us to recall these things so that all may understand that We, despite the fact that new conditions of the times and of affairs have moved Us to grant not a few faculties and favors on this subject, still wish through this apostolic letter to confirm the supreme force of the law and custom dealing with the Eucharistic fast; and that We wish also to admonish those who are able to observe that same law that they should continue diligently to observe it, so that only those who need these concessions can enjoy them according to the nature of their need."

That is to say: the principle of the Eucharistic fast remains intact. But adaptations in its application are called for in our day, lest the faithful be prevented from partaking of the divine mysteries.

Thereupon the Holy Father enumerates the new changes under six headings. But in concluding he again states emphatically: "In granting these faculties which the conditions of persons, places and times demand today, We ardently desire to emphasize the force and the value of the Eucharistic fast for those who are able to receive our Divine Redeemer hidden under the Eucharistic veils." And he does not fail to add that, to the extent that bodily fasting is mitigated, "the soul must supply [the equivalent] as far as it can, either by internal penance or by other means," especially by fervent prayers and by increased fruits of charity towards neighbor.

To understand better this inner, organic relation between fasting and reception of the Eucharist, it will be useful to recall some data of history. Pope Pius XII reminds us that the Eucharistic fast was customary since earliest times, even though it became matter of more universal legislation only towards the end of the fourth century, about the time of St. Augustine.

Now I personally believe that the Eucharistic fast cannot be properly understood, or evaluated, if viewed *in isolation*. Rather, because the Eucharist is the first and most noble sacrament, the Eucharistic fast offers the most important instance of a general rule: namely, that great spiritual happenings, or feasts, should be prepared for spiritually, by prayer and fasting. Before we draw near to the Divinity, we must humble ourselves, prepare ourselves, dispose ourselves. And fasting was recognized as a good preparation even by pagans.[1] Historians cite innumerable examples. And of course the Old Testament likewise abounds in illustrations. In fact, the Jews at the time of Christ fasted before partaking of the paschal meal—and some authors see

---

[1] Cf. R. Arbesmann, *Das Fasten bei den Griechen und Römern* (Giessen, 1929).

in this Jewish custom the immediate source of the Christian practice of the Eucharistic fast.[2]

This sound religious instinct, of fasting and mortification, to prepare for God's acts of mercy, found its highest possible realization in Christianity. The mystery of Christianity is the mystery of Christ's death and resurrection. His death as our way to eternal life is the sum and essence of the Christian dispensation. Now the Eucharist is the making present again of Christ's death and resurrection for every generation. And so likewise is every sacrament an effective sign of that saving death and new life. In fact, every outpouring of divine grace, what is it but the operation of Christ's death and rising? For, as St. Paul says, "Christ was delivered up for our sins, and rose again for our justification" (Rom. 4:25).

Hence, active sharing in Christ's grace, in His life, presupposes a previous active sharing in His passion and death on our part. We, too, must first die with Christ, if we wish to live with Him. We must die with Him to sin: bodily fasting, which is, as it were, a quasi-dying, was therefore considered from earliest times a necessary guarantee of the sincerity of man's determination to turn away from sin. By fasting, man, to a certain extent, bore the passion of Christ in his own body.

This explains why fasting has been customary to a greater or lesser degree, not only before receiving the Eucharist, but also before receiving other Sacraments, and before some of the great Sacramentals as well.

Thus fasting before baptism, though never so rigorous nor so general as the Eucharistic fast, has an ancient and strong tradition. In the *Didache*, one of the earliest Christian writings, we read: "Before baptism, let him who baptizes and him who is to be baptized fast; and all others who are able. But you should command the candidate to fast one or two days" (ch. 7). And St. Justin, writing about the middle of the second century, says: Candidates (for baptism) should fast "in order to effect the remission of their former sins. And we fast and pray with them" (*1 Apol.* 61). Even to our own time, canon law decrees: "It is

---

[2] E.g., J. Schuemmer, *Die Altchristliche Fastenpraxis* [Liturgiegeschichtliche Quellen und Forschungen, 27] (Muenster i. Westf., 1933), pp. 70 ff.

fitting that both the priest who is to baptize adults, and these adults themselves if they are in good health, should be fasting" (Can. 753, 1).—In regard to *confirmation*: this sacrament was originally conferred together with baptism, so the same law of fasting applied as for baptism. Later, a special law for fasting before confirmation was introduced, but did not maintain itself.[3]—As to the sacrament of *penance*: the season of Lenten fasting of forty days had the original meaning of atonement for sins committed, in preparation for the reconciliation or absolution on the Thursday before Easter. Its association with the paschal (baptismal) mystery was a subsequent development.

The sacrament of *holy orders*, too, has traditionally been prepared for by prayer and fasting. Thus we read in the Acts of the Apostles: "And as they were ministering to the Lord and fasting, the Holy Spirit said: 'Set apart for me Saul and Barnabas unto the work to which I have called them.' Then, having fasted and prayed, and laid their hands upon them, they let them go" (13:2–3). And again: "When they (Paul and Barnabas) had appointed presbyters for them in each church, with prayer and fasting they commended them to the Lord" (14:22). This tradition has left its echo to our own day: for the four ember Saturdays, fast days, are days of ordination. It would be a good idea, incidentally, to remind our people of this fact, that they offer up the fast and abstinence of the ember days for a good harvest of newly ordained priests.

The *consecration of a bishop*, likewise, is prepared for by fasting. In the Pontifical, the rubric introducing the rite of consecration reads: "It is fitting that the consecrating bishops as well as the bishop-elect fast on the day preceding the consecration." There is a similar rubric, moreover, for the blessing of an abbot, and also for the great parish event of the consecration of a church. In the latter case, the rubric reads: "When a church is to be dedicated, let this be announced to the clergy and the people for whom the church is to be consecrated, in order that they may fast before the consecration. For the consecrating bishop and those who asked to have their church con-

[3] Cf. Abbot F. Cabrol, O.S.B., article "Jeûnes" in *Dictionnaire d'Archéologie Chrétienne et de Liturgie*, c. 2487.

secrated should fast on the preceding day." And of course we all know how the greatest feasts of the year, i.e., the days of greatest grace, are prepared for by entire seasons, or at least by individual vigil days, of fasting.

All of this is simply another way of stating the classical Christian arguments motivating the fast: it overcomes Satan, it atones for sin, and it prepares for the coming of the Holy Ghost, the Sanctifier.

But since the Eucharist is the center and summary of the whole sacramental system, fasting was always most rigorously and widely observed in its case. In fact, for many centuries, the faithful were commanded to be fasting for *attendance at holy Mass,* even though they did not communicate. We have evidence of this as late as the fifteenth century. Thus, in an important synod at Brixen, in 1453, a law was promulgated for bidding taverns to offer anything by way of food or drink until after the main Mass in the town had been celebrated.[4] This fasting for Mass, even without Communion, was really an edifying way to participate actively in the sacrifice: by bodily mortification the people expressed their readiness to share in the sacrificial passion of Christ. It was also, by the way, a good means of uniting priest and people in the sacrificial offering. The people were reminded that, since the priest offers in their name, they should, as he, be properly prepared and disposed by fasting.[5]

To summarize: the principle of the Eucharistic fast is not to be viewed in isolation. It is in its origin and in its purposes simply the most important example of a general rule of the spiritual life: that death to self and to sin is the only path to receiving

[4] Peter Browe, S.J., "Die Nüchternheit vor der Messe und Kommunion im Mittelalter," in *Ephemerides Liturgicae,* XLV (1931), 281.

[5] Cf. A. Franz, *Die Messe im deutschen Mittelalter* (Freiburg im Br., 1902), pp. 62 ff., who cites one of the decrees of the Brixen synod: "*Sicut enim celebrans debet esse jejunus, ita et audientes, quia, ut canon dicit, simul cum ipso sacerdote hostiam offerunt.*" Less correct was another motiviation often proposed during these centuries of infrequent people's Communion: that the priest receives Holy Communion in the congregation's name and stead, and hence the faithful too should fast. Cf. J. A. Jungmann, S.J., *Missarum Sollemnia,* II, p. 443.

an abundant outpouring of divine life. We therefore fast from natural food as our preparation for receiving the Bread of Life. For unless we are willing to die with Christ, we cannot hope to live with Him.

This all seems obvious enough. Yet we know that this chief meaning and purpose of the Eucharistic fast is *not* the chief reason in most people's minds today. If I were to ask an average Catholic audience why we should fast before Holy Communion, I think I would get some such answer as this: "We fast out of reverence. For it is hardly reverent to Christ to receive other food before receiving His Sacred Body and Blood." Now this is not a wrong answer. But it is only a partial answer. And if it is the only answer in people's minds, it can easily lead to wrong conclusions in practice. It can even keep people away from Holy Communion.

Actually, that is precisely what did happen for nearly 1400 years, until Pope Pius X's decree on frequent Communion. The legislation about the Eucharistic fast at the end of the fourth and during the fifth century coincided with the anti-Arian struggle, first in the East, and then against the semi-Arian barbarians, in the West, as described in the Introduction. The heretic Arius had denied that Christ was true God. In reaction, St. Basil and St. John Chrysostom, among others, stressed the divinity of Christ, not only theologically, as a doctrine, but also in practice, in divine worship. The Holy Eucharist, instead of a love feast, a supper of union with Christ our brother, became the awful, *mysterium tremendum,* in which the Son of God becomes present in our midst. And who, except the most pure and most holy, would dare approach to receive Him? Emphasis was placed on the divinity of the person of Christ in the Eucharist, rather than on the fact that the Eucharist is a sacred food to help us in our spiritual weakness.

As a consequence, reception of Holy Communion, which was a normal part of assistance at Mass until well into the fourth century, now quickly became a rare event. So rare, indeed, that people had to be forced to go to Communion at least once a year. And this emphasis on the divinity of Christ in the Eucharist found its counterpart in the reasons given for the Eucharistic fast. The stomach should be empty of all other food out of reverence for the Divine Guest to be received[6]—that became more or less the *exclusive* motivation for the fast.

It seems to me, therefore, to be of considerable importance that we again get a fuller and more adequate understanding of the Eucharistic fast. The purpose of the Eucharistic fast is to prepare us to receive Holy Communion, not to keep us away from it!

Reverence, yes. The Lord knows we have almost forgotten the meaning of the word. But more is required: a vivid realization that Christ comes to us in Holy Communion, not primarily as our God to be reverently adored, but in order to transform us into Himself. And He is the Victim on the cross: "And I, if I be lifted up," He said of Himself, "shall draw all things to myself" (John 12:32). For us to desire to receive the life of Christ in Holy Communion without our having joined ourselves first to the sacrifice of Christ means to be parasites of the altar. We must be on the altar, not merely at the altar.

The Eucharistic fast is a means to an end: that we may partake more fully in the sacrifice and in its fruit, Holy Communion. Modern conditions of life hindered the fast from achieving its end. Hence, some details in the rule of fast had to be changed. Nor can we be grateful enough to Pius XII for having introduced those changes. Frequent Communion is our goal. Bishop Dworschak of Fargo interpreted the mind of the Holy Father correctly, I believe, when he told his priests that they have a grave obligation to make available to their people every advantage the new apostolic constitution offers.[7] The laity should be encouraged to ask for mitigation of the fast when-

---

[6] This was interpreted strictly: hence not only fasting was demanded, but also a previous night's sleep and total digestion of the previous evening's meal, i.e., emptiness of stomach and bowels. Browe (*op. cit.*, pp. 284 f.) cites a papal letter, decrees of synods, and pertinent arguments voiced by liturgists and canonists, from the twelfth to the fifteenth centuries. Such a one-sided stress on the reverence motif also resulted in synodal decrees legislating a Eucharistic fast of several days, or abstinence from meat for various periods of time, and likewise contributed to a multiplication of the days when abstaining from marital intercourse was urged before receiving the Blessed Sacrament. Cf. Jungmann, *op. cit.*, pp. 441 f.

[7] Cf. *Worship* (July, 1953), 390.

ever such mitigation makes it more reasonably possible for them to receive the Holy Eucharist.

But frequency of reception is not the whole goal. Mere multiplication of Communions is in itself no guarantee of spiritual growth. Frequent *worthy* reception is the whole goal. But worthy reception means, necessarily, the spirit of sacrifice. And that, according to the constant teaching and practice of the Church, entails, *normally*, also the bodily sacrifice of fasting. "I exhort you, therefore, brethren, by the mercy of God," St. Paul tells us, "to present your bodies as a sacrifice, holy, pleasing to God" (Rom. 12:1). Hence Pius XII's insistence that the changes in the rules of fasting do not lessen or obscure the principle of the Eucharistic fast. And he further insists that the more bodily fasting is mitigated in practice, the more urgently we must prepare ourselves by increased internal penance.

IV. THE LITURGY AND EDUCATION

As a theologian, on the one hand, yet treating in this chapter, on the other hand, matters of particular interest also to Protestant readers, I feel that I can most profitably treat my subject from the theological point of view, but limiting myself strictly to the data of Scripture and to the very earliest Christian writings, i.e., the so-called Apostolic Fathers: the two letters to the Corinthians attributed to Clement, the seven letters of Ignatius of Antioch, Polycarp's epistle and the eye-witness account of his martyrdom, and finally the Epistle to Diognetus. These writings are our common and precious heritage; the Scriptures are for all of us the inspired word of God. Perhaps therefore an analysis of their teaching concerning the nature and purpose and characteristics of the Christian community which we call a "parish" may throw some valuable light on our subject.

Moreover I have restricted myself entirely to the philological

Reprinted from "The Church-Related College and the Parish," *Association of American Colleges Bulletin*, XLI (May, 1955) 246–56.

and historical approach to the theological concepts at issue. In such an approach every theologian, whether Catholic or Protestant, will find indispensable help in that monument of Protestant biblical scholarship, the *Theologisches Wörterbuch zum Neuen Testament,* begun by Gerhard Kittel and after his death continued (it is not yet complete) by Gerhard Friedrich and a group of learned associates. In all the chief points at issue in this chapter there was substantial agreement between the findings of this work of scholarship and the conclusions of Catholic specialists in the field, such as Alfred Wikenhauser and Franz Xaver Arnold in Germany and Ferdinand Prat in France.

I have accordingly restricted my argument to such theological data as is commonly accepted by leading Christian scholars. I believe that the presentation of these generally accepted principles can prove remarkably fruitful for assisting us in arriving at some conclusions in the practical order. After all, it has been discovered more than once that sound principles often prove unexpectedly practical.

The very wording of the subject, "The Church-Related College and the Parish," reveals a manner of thinking which I believe is quite general whether among Catholics or Protestants. "Church" and "parish," according to our usual way of speaking, are related to each other as the whole to its part. The Church is the whole; the parish its part, existing in a certain locality. Now the first question I would like to raise is: Does this common interpretation of the words correspond fully to the data of Scripture and the earliest Christian writings? And if not, can the original, scriptural meaning help us to grasp our subject better and to arrive at practical conclusions in our discussion?

The Greek original in the New Testament for our word "church" is *ekklesia.* It was already used in the Septuagint, the pre-Christian Greek translation of the Old Testament, to designate the community of Jews in any city in their role of chosen people, chosen and called by God to pay Him faithful worship. It meant therefore, first of all, the local community of true worshipers.

It is in this sense of a local community of true believers and worshipers that the word *ekklesia* (or church) was most frequently used also in the New Testament. The apostle Paul, for example, greets the "Church of God at Corinth" (I Cor. 1:2; II Cor. 1:2), he speaks of "the Church at Cenchrae" (Rom. 16:1), of "the Church of the Thessalonians" (I Thess. 1:1; II Thess. 1:1). No less than twenty times he refers in the plural to "the Church of Asia," "of Galatia," "of the Macedonians," "of Judaea," etc. Again he speaks of the "Churches of the saints" or of "all the Churches everywhere."

In other words, if we judge by the frequency with which the word "church" was employed, it would seem to designate, in most instances, not the entire or universal Church but the local community of Christians: not the whole, but the part.

However, it is used to designate the whole Church some 17 times in all, and of these 17 instances 11 are to be found in Colossians and Ephesians, in which Paul develops his thought most clearly concerning the Church as the body of Christ.

It would not then be according to the mind of Scripture simply to identify the word "church" with the concept of the universal Church in contradistinction to its local realization. This is all the more evident if we recall that Paul used the word "church" even in referring to a very small group of Christians, meeting (ostensibly for worship) in a private home. Thus he twice sends greetings to the "Church that is in the house" of his co-workers Prisca and Aquila at Rome (Rom. 16:5; I Cor. 16:19), to the "Church that is in the house of Nymphas" at Laodicea (Col. 4:15) and to the Church in the house of Philemon (Philemon 2).

According to this use of terms, therefore, the local community is not merely a geographical division of the universal Church, but in its own way it represents the whole Church; it is somehow a concrete realization of the whole, the Church in miniature. For this reason Paul, in I Cor. 12, in trying to allay the divisions and schisms which had occurred in the Corinth community of Christians, could and does apply to the local community arguments drawn from the concept of the entire Church as the body of Christ: "Now you are the body of Christ, and individually parts of it" (I Cor. 12:27).

To summarize, we have here something like the figure of speech called synecdoche: the part stands for the whole, and the whole is in some manner contained in the part.

Limiting ourselves to this data, borne out further in the writings of Clement, Ignatius and Polycarp, we may deduce some conclusions in the practical order.

The first and most important would seem to be that the individual Christian experiences the Church above all in his local community. The parish is for him, in a true sense of the word even if not in the fullest sense of the word, the Christian Church to which he belongs. In the providence of God, the individual normally belongs to the Church because he belongs to, is a member of, this local community of believers and worshipers. He exercises his membership in the universal Church immediately and primarily (though not exclusively) by exercising his membership in *this* church, which is the parish. It is in the parish, the Church in miniature, that he normally receives the benefits which the Church has to offer: in other words, where he grows in Christ.

If church-related colleges, then, have the duty of preparing their students to take a responsible part in the life and work of the Church, this necessarily and most immediately means preparing them for better active membership in their respective parishes. The family and the local Christian community (the parish) call upon the college to assist them in the formation and training of one of their members; they as it were "loan" him for a number of years to the college. Unless the college, therefore, succeeds in developing among its students a proper parish consciousness and parish loyalty, and an enlightened sense of responsibility for future work in the parish, it will have failed in its most immediate task as a church-related college.

To sum up: the problem of church-related colleges and the parish is not merely a secondary aspect of our specific program as Christian schools: rather it embodies something that is of the essence of our *raison d'être*.

How such a parish awareness can be developed in a college, whether in religion classes by stressing the true meaning of a parish and pointing our instruction to participation in parish life, or by more frequently inviting pastors to speak to our students, or by whatever other means, will, I suppose, be matter for discussion. What I have tried to do so far is to show, theologically, the basic relevance of the problem to the program of church-related colleges.

Next in order logically is a theological analysis of the concept of "local community" or parish. For if the college is to prepare its students for parish life, a better understanding of the main characteristics of parish life, such as the inspired word of God presents them, will be imperative. I intend to develop this line of thought under three headings: (1) the parish as a community of the chosen people whose true citizenship is in heaven; (2) some chief traits of Christian living in a community; (3) personal responsibility and Christian maturity of the individual.

1. *The parish as a community of the chosen people whose true citizenship is in heaven.*

We have seen earlier that the word *ekklesia* (or church) was used in the New Testament most frequently, though not exhaustively, to signify the local Christian community. But there is another word which, while not so prominent in New Testament usage, already in the non-scriptural writings of the first century after Christ became in the strictest sense a technical term for this same idea of a local community of Christians. That word is the noun *paroikia* (and its adjective form *paroikos* and its verb form *paroikeo*). From it derives, obviously, our English word "parish" (and its counterparts in other modern European languages: *Pfarrei, paroisse, parrocchia*). In fact this Greek word *paroikia* is found only in Scriptural and Christian usage and not in profane writings of the time—which fact heightens its significance for us.

Paroikia, and its adjective and verb forms, occurs eight times in the New Testament. In each case there is question either of a direct quotation from, or an allusion to, an Old Testament passage. A very brief analysis of its very frequent Septuagint use is therefore in order.

Generally speaking, *paroikos* in the Old Testament is the equivalent of the Hebrew *Ger,* meaning stranger or non-citizen. Abraham is a stranger in Egypt, so are the chosen people. Isaac was a stranger in Canaan, Lot in Sodom, etc. *Paroikos,* then, means a resident in a certain locality who does not have full rights of citizenship. The entire chosen people are often so called, even (and this is significant) while they dwelt in the promised land. God reminds them repeatedly that they are *paroikoi*, strangers, residents without permanent rights, even in their own homeland (cf. I Chron. 29:15), in order to make them realize that He alone is the sole and absolute Lord and Proprietor of all they possess (cf. Lev. 25:23). They are only stewards of the land, which really belongs to God.

What the Old Testament said of Israel, that the New Testament transferred to the saints of the Church of God. We all know some of the New Testament passages: e.g., I Pet. 2:11: "Dearly beloved, I beseech you *as strangers and pilgrims,* abstain from fleshly lust"; Hebr. 13:14: "For here we have no abiding city, but we seek one to come." More important, however, the New Testament is not merely negative. While insisting on our condition of pilgrims and strangers on earth, it reveals the good tidings that we are even on earth true "fellow citizens with the saints, and of the household of God" (Eph. 2:19).

We find this use of *paroikos* or *paroikia* subsequently taken up by all the very earliest Christian writings. Harnack states: "The words 'strangers and pilgrims' became almost technical terms for the Christians of the first century to designate themselves; while the word *paroikia* (which in Scripture meant the condition of being a pilgrim, and was applied either to the entire community or to an individual member of it) did become in the strictest sense a technical term for the local community of Christians in the world" (*Mission und Ausbreitung des Christentums,* I [1906], p. 421, footnote). *Paroikia* became from very early times, therefore, the exact synonym for the local church or community, whereas the word *ekklesia* came to be used more and more of the universal Church.

This means that a parish, to be a true Christian community according to Scripture, must realize, in its faith and in its activities, its own title of *paroikia,* a community of pilgrims: i.e., it must be a community in which the awareness of being citizens of heaven outweighs, and therefore governs and directs, the members' concern for the things of earth. It means that they must not be a community of spiritual bourgeois, of people who feel unabashedly at home in the world. It means stirring up that divine discontent which Augustine had in mind when he said: "Our hearts are restless until they rest in Thee." It means a certain emphasis on the eschatological aspect of Christianity— a topic, by the way, concerning which we may recall that the World Council of Churches had some interesting things to say at Evanston in 1954.

Among the early Christian writers, the author of the Epistle to Diognetus summed it up most effectively in a famous passage:

"Christians are not distinguished from the rest of mankind by either country, speech or customs; the fact is, they nowhere settle down in cities of their own; they use no peculiar language; they cultivate no eccentric mode of life. Certainly this creed of theirs is no discovery due to some fancy or speculation of inquisitive men; nor do they, as some do, champion a doctrine of human origin. Yet while they dwell in both Greek and non-Greek cities, as each one's lot was cast, and conform to the customs of the country in dress, food and mode of life in general, the whole tenor of their way of living stamps it as worthy of admiration and admittedly extraordinary. They reside in their respective countries, but as aliens. They take part in everything as citizens and put up with everything as foreigners. Every foreign land is their home, and every home a foreign land (5:1-5)."

To cultivate such a mentality is not an easy task, to be sure, either for a parish or for a church-related college preparing its students for parish life. For we are living in a secularist age. Yet the task is inherent not only in the word "parish" but also in the word "Church," which signifies those chosen by God, set apart from among others in order to serve Him.

There is perhaps no need to point out that this insistence on being strangers and pilgrims on earth does not involve an unconcern for the world, or anything like escapism. The same author of the Epistle to Diognetus, immediately after the passage just quoted, says: "In a word, what the soul is in the body, that the Christians are in the world" (6:1). And we have Christ's example of love, not only for men but for inanimate nature as well, His predilection for mountains and lakes, etc., and His explicit command that we must be a leaven that changes the world, a light that enlightens others. It is clearly obvious to all of us that we cannot love God and despise the hem of His garment. Or again we have the magnificent second-century example of Justin Martyr's attitude to pagan philosophies.

What this Christian paradox of "being in the world but not of the world" ultimately adds up to, I suppose, is nothing else than a matter of developing a true sense of values. Someone has defined education as an inculcation of an informed sensitivity to values. And our values must, realistically, include God. Why do church-related colleges exist? Merely to teach religion as a separate course? Or rather in the light of eternal and divine values to teach a complete *Weltanschauung*: to show our pupils how, by being good citizens of the household of God, they can and must be better temporary citizens of the world? If our church-related colleges turn out graduates who, except for some spare moments devoted to prayer or worship, are as secularist in their daily outlook as the next man, then we should close our doors. Then we are public and criminal frauds, getting money under false pretenses. Our chief enemy today is radical secularism—of which Communism is but the most virulent manifestation. Training for parish life means giving our students an insight into the corrosive character of secularism, teaching them to recognize it (and that often is the crux), to be on their guard against it and to overcome it in themselves and help their fellow parishioners to overcome it by making the higher values decisive in their living.

Would it be out of place to suggest that the ideal of respectability, too, can become an insidious form of secularism? To an appalling degree, the cult of respectability is threatening to substitute for the cult of Yahweh.

T. S. Eliot has perhaps given us the most incisive picture of a secularist civilization:

A cry from the North, from the West and from the South
Whence thousands travel daily to the timekept City;
Where My Word is unspoken.
In the land of lobelias and tennis flannels
The rabbit shall burrow and the thorn revisit,
The nettle shall flourish on the gravel court,

And the wind shall say: 'Here were decent godless people:
Their only monument the asphalt road
And a thousand lost golf balls' (*The Rock*).

Decent godless people. How can we prevent our students
from becoming such and later, as leaders in their parish, from
corrupting others to become such? By developing a true sense of
values, in which God occupies first place. But how? Can we
make the religion course the integrating factor of our school?
Besides religion, are there other courses which church-related
colleges must especially stress and should demand of all their
students, courses which of their nature impart a greater sense
of values, such as history, philosophy, the classics? And must
these be taught differently in a church-related college? Are we
giving a false sense of values to our students by trying too hard
to keep up with the Joneses in the extravagance of our physical
plants, or in letting money talk too loudly in determining some
of our policies? I ask questions. Perhaps they are unduly naïve.
But I am only a theologian. I gladly leave the practical matters
to more practical people.

2. *Some chief traits of Christian living in a community.* The
parish is not merely a sum total of individuals but a community.
It is in miniature the Body of Christ, in which the members belong to each other as truly as they belong to Christ. The apostle
Paul in I Cor. 12 has given us the classic description of such a
body, of such a community, in which the foot cannot say to the
hand "I have no need of thee." The author of the Acts, too, tells
us of the first communities of Christians, how they were all of
one accord in prayer and supplication (Acts 1:14). I could cite
numerous pertinent passages from the earliest Christian writings,
but sufficiently decisive for all of us is Christ's command to His
community of apostles at the Last Supper: "By this shall all men
know that you are my disciples, that you have love one for
another." It might however be of interest to know that this
command of our Saviour was so well carried out in the first
generations that a synonym for local church was the word *agape*,
meaning charity (cf. Ignatius of Antioch).

The parish community, accordingly, is the community of
Christian life and worship and of mutual love. The individual

Christian, in the normal course of events, takes part in the Church's life by taking part in the community's activities, by receiving from the community, by contributing to it. He experiences the Church, the Body of Christ, by experiencing the community.

If I may hazard to spell out some of the requirements for a community life, perhaps the following might be mentioned: (1) the sense of belonging to a group and the conviction of somehow being important to this group, i.e., of being more than a mere cipher; (2) a feeling of responsibility for the needs of the group, which in turn involves (3) an understanding of the purpose of the group and of its problems; (4) a willingness to collaborate on a friendly basis and not to seek one's own benefit at the expense of the group. There are other qualities, of course, but these may suffice for the present.

Since the church-related college prepares its students for parish life, it must provide an opportunity for continuing and even deepening their sense and experience of Christian community life and worship. How big can a college get without losing its community character? Already Plato in his *Republic* wrestled with the same problem in terms of the city state. Perhaps the only answer is a relative one: a community ceases to exist as a real community when personal relations between its members cease to be the norm. Certainly, indefinite expansion does not seem reconcilable with the aims of a church-related college. If the college is already too large, every effort must be expended to give the students the experience of a community on a lower level, perhaps on the basis of the individual dormitory buildings. I would think too that this effort at community living would have to express itself even in such a field as athletics: that there be a greater emphasis on intramural sports, to give more members an opportunity of participating—although I would be the last to deny that a winning varsity team also can help to engender a school or community spirit. Moreover a college, with its faculty and students, has a certain similarity to a parish, with its leader or leaders and its congregation. Closer faculty-student bonds must accordingly be one of our ideals: the instructor in a church-related college may not be an autocrat at the teacher's table but must be motivated by the spirit of Christian ministry or service. "I came not to be ministered unto but to minister."

All these things are obvious enough and similar practical conclusions can be multiplied easily. May I however add two final thoughts. Firstly, Christian community spirit is not the same as mere humanitarianism. The decent godless people can and not infrequently do surpass us in friendly courtesy and kindness. Genuine Christian community life is due to the virtue of charity —which means loving our neighbor because of our love of God. "Whatever you have done to the least of these, you have done unto Me." It must therefore find its inspiration in Christian community worship—hence an additional reason for the importance of the latter in church-related colleges. Secondly, while charity begins at home, it should not end there. A parish community, though it represents the entire Church, is not the universal Church. Community charity must therefore not be hemmed in by parish boundaries. St. Paul, who addressed the Christian community of Thessalonica as "the Church of the Thessalonians," urged this community nevertheless to extend its charity in alms to the Christians of Jerusalem. Yet experience amply demonstrates how self-centered a parish can become—a fact borne out by the word "parochialism." Perhaps a special task of the church-related college consists therefore in widening the vision and interest of its students to include more clearly the needs of the whole Church, its missions, etc.—in the hope that upon their return home they will be able to share that broader vision with their fellow parishioners.

3. *Personal responsibility and the Christian maturity of the individual.*

The concepts "community" and "person" are dynamite. Their extremes, collectivism (or statism) and individualism, are two opposing poles and the whole of human history could be written in terms of a pendulum swinging uneasily, and often violently, from one to the other. We know how, in spite of Christian emphasis on community, it has been Christianity which has at the same time proclaimed and defended the inalienable, God-given rights of the individual. The Christian community may not absorb the individual but must be the framework in which the individual is enabled to arrive at the full stature of Christ.

"It is not good for man to be alone." He achieves his fullest development of personality by working in and with and for the community.

The ultimate proof of this paradoxical fact is found in the life of the Blessed Trinity itself, of which man and mankind are the image and likeness. According to traditional teaching, first enunciated by Augustine, the personality of each divine Person in the Trinity is constituted by, consists in, His relation to another Person, or to both other Persons: we might say, in His giving Himself to the Other. Does not this imply, in terms of Christian life, that the Christian person most effectively develops his Christian personality by serving others—and by a corresponding forgetfulness of self? The divine mathematics are different from our human brand. "He who loses his life shall find it."

This, it seems to me, would in turn postulate two things: (1) *firstly* that the student be explicitly and often encouraged to contribute to the well-being of the community, and also that opportunity be provided for him to do so—this would, preferably, find its first and best expression in the sphere of community worship; (2) *secondly* that individual initiative be given the widest possible scope consonant with the school's aims, and with school discipline. The entire question of student councils or student government would come under this heading.

In the Catholic Church the emphasis on such lay initiative and responsibility has in recent years found expression in what is known as Catholic Action and, in the field of worship, in the so-called liturgical movement. Other churches and local communities will have their own practical efforts at answers according to their respective polity. In every event, the church-related school may not remain unconcernedly aloof from the problem. Four years of passivity, even in the form of mere receptivity in the classroom, of allowing oneself patiently to be lectured at, are not the optimum preparation for adult Christian responsibility in parish life.

INDEX

* Prepared by Father Benjamin J. Stein, O.S.B., chairman of the Library Science Section of the American Benedictine Academy.

Image Books

OUR LADY OF FATIMA
By William Thomas Walsh
D1—75¢

THE SPIRIT OF CATHOLICISM
By Karl Adam   D2—85¢

DAMIEN THE LEPER
By John Farrow   D3—85¢

**A POPULAR HISTORY OF THE
CATHOLIC CHURCH**
By Philip Hughes   D4—95¢

MR. BLUE
By Myles Connolly   D5—65¢

THE DIARY OF A COUNTRY PRIEST
By Georges Bernanos D6—75¢

**THE CHURCH SPEAKS TO THE
MODERN WORLD:**
*The Social Teachings of Leo
XIII. Edited by Etienne Gilson*
D7—95¢

PEACE OF SOUL
By Fulton J. Sheen   D8—85¢

LIFT UP YOUR HEART
By Fulton J. Sheen   D9—85¢

STORM OF GLORY
*The Story of St. Thérèse of
Lisieux. By John Beevers*
D10—75¢

THE PERFECT JOY OF ST. FRANCIS
By Felix Timmermans
D11—85¢

SAINTS FOR OUR TIMES
By Theodore Maynard
D12—95¢

**INTRODUCTION TO THE DEVOUT
LIFE**
*By St. Francis de Sales. Newly
translated and edited by John
K. Ryan*   D13—95¢

THE ROAD TO DAMASCUS
Edited by John A. O'Brien
D14—85¢

**JOYCE KILMER'S ANTHOLOGY OF
CATHOLIC POETS**
*With a new supplement by
James Edward Tobin*
D15—$1.25

BERNADETTE AND LOURDES
By Michel de Saint-Pierre
D16—85¢

THE IMITATION OF CHRIST
By Thomas à Kempis. A Modern Version edited with an Introduction by Harold C. Gardiner, S.J.   D17—85¢

THE EVERLASTING MAN
By G. K. Chesterton D18—95¢

A GRAMMAR OF ASSENT
*By John Henry Cardinal Newman with an Introduction by
Etienne Gilson*   D19—$1.25

BROTHER PETROC'S RETURN
By S. M. C.   D21—75¢

ST. FRANCIS OF ASSISI
By Johannes Jörgensen
D22—95¢

**STORIES OF OUR CENTURY BY
CATHOLIC AUTHORS**
Edited by John Gilland Brunini and Francis X. Connolly
D23—95¢

**AUTOBIOGRAPHY OF A HUNTED
PRIEST**
*By John Gerard. Introduction
by Graham Greene*   D24—95¢

FATHER MALACHY'S MIRACLE
By Bruce Marshall   D25—75¢

**ON THE TRUTH OF THE CATHOLIC
FAITH**   *Summa Contra Gentiles Book I: God. Newly translated, with Introduction and
notes by Anton C. Pegis*
D26—95¢

Image Books

... MAKING THE WORLD'S FINEST
CATHOLIC LITERATURE AVAILABLE TO ALL

**ON THE TRUTH OF THE
CATHOLIC FAITH**
*Summa Contra Gentiles Book II:
Creation. Newly translated, with
an Introduction and notes by
James F. Anderson* D27—95¢

**ON THE TRUTH OF THE
CATHOLIC FAITH**
*Summa Contra Gentiles Book
III: Providence. Newly trans-
lated, with an Introduction and
notes by Vernon J. Bourke*
  D28a Book III, Part 1—95¢
  D28b Book III, Part 2—95¢

**ON THE TRUTH OF THE
CATHOLIC FAITH**
*Summa Contra Gentiles Book
IV: Salvation. Newly translated,
with an Introduction and notes.
By Charles J. O'Neill* D29—95¢

THE WORLD'S FIRST LOVE
By Fulton J. Sheen D30—85¢

THE SIGN OF JONAS
By Thomas Merton D31—95¢

**PARENTS, CHILDREN AND THE
FACTS OF LIFE**
Sattler, C.S.S.R.   D32—75¢

LIGHT ON THE MOUNTAIN:
*The Story of La Salette
By John S. Kennedy* D33—75¢

EDMUND CAMPION
By Evelyn Waugh D34—75¢

HUMBLE POWERS
By Paul Horgan   D35—75¢

SAINT THOMAS AQUINAS
By G. K. Chesterton D36—75¢

APOLOGIA PRO VITA SUA
*By John Henry Cardinal New-
man Introduction by Philip
Hughes*   D37—95¢

**A HANDBOOK OF THE CATHOLIC
FAITH**
*By Dr. N. G. M. Van Doornik,
Rev. S. Jelsma, Rev. A. Van De
Lisdonk. Ed. Rev. John Green-
wood*   D38—$1.55

THE NEW TESTAMENT
Official Catholic edition
  D39—95¢

MARIA CHAPDELAINE
By Louis Hémon D40—65¢

SAINT AMONG THE HURONS
By Francis X. Talbot, S.J.
  D41—95¢

THE PATH TO ROME
By Hilaire Belloc D42—85¢

SORROW BUILT A BRIDGE
By Katherine Burton D43—85¢

THE WISE MAN FROM THE WEST
By Vincent Cronin D44—85¢

EXISTENCE AND THE EXISTENT
By Jacques Maritain D45—75¢

**THE STORY OF THE TRAPP
FAMILY SINGERS**
By Maria Augusta Trapp
  D46—95¢

**THE WORLD, THE FLESH AND
FATHER SMITH**
By Bruce Marshall D47—75¢

THE CHRIST OF CATHOLICISM
By Dom Aelred Graham
  D48—95¢

SAINT FRANCIS XAVIER
By James Brodrick, S.J.
  D49—95¢

SAINT FRANCIS OF ASSISI
By G. K. Chesterton D50—75¢

Image Books

*...making the world's finest
Catholic literature available to all*

VIPERS' TANGLE
by François Mauriac D51—75¢

THE MANNER IS ORDINARY
by John LaFarge, S.J. D52—95¢

MY LIFE FOR MY SHEEP
by Alfred Duggan D53—90¢

THE CHURCH AND THE RECON-
STRUCTION OF THE MODERN
WORLD: *The Social Encyclicals
of Pius XI.* Edited by T. P. Mc-
Laughlin, C.S.B. D54—$1.25

A GILSON READER: *Selections from
the Writings of Etienne Gilson.*
Edited by Anton C. Pegis.
D55—$1.25

THE AUTOBIOGRAPHY OF
ST. THERESE OF LISIEUX: *The Story
of a Soul.* A new translation by
John Beevers. D56—75¢

HELENA
by Evelyn Waugh D57—75¢

THE GREATEST BIBLE STORIES
A Catholic Anthology from
World Literature. Edited by Anne
Fremantle. D58—75¢

THE CITY OF GOD—St. Augustine.
Edited with Intro. by Vernon J.
Bourke. Foreword by Etienne
Gilson. D59—$1.55

SUPERSTITION CORNER
by Sheila Kaye-Smith D60—65¢

SAINTS AND OURSELVES
Ed. by Philip Caraman, S.J.
D61—95¢

CANA IS FOREVER
by Charles Hugo Doyle
D62—85¢

ASCENT OF MOUNT CARMEL—
St. John of the Cross. Translated
and Edited by E. Allison Peers.
D63—$1.25

RELIGION AND THE RISE OF
WESTERN CULTURE
by Christopher Dawson
D64—85¢

PRINCE OF DARKNESS AND OTHER
STORIES
by J. F. Powers D65—85¢

ST. THOMAS MORE
by E. E. Reynolds D66—95¢

JESUS AND HIS TIMES
2 Volumes D67A—95¢
by Daniel-Rops D67B—95¢

ST. BENEDICT
by Justin McCann, O.S.B.
D68—85¢

THE LITTLE FLOWERS OF ST. FRANCIS
Edited and Translated by
Raphael Brown. D69—95¢

THE QUIET LIGHT
by Louis de Wohl D70—95¢

CHARACTERS OF THE REFORMATION
by Hilaire Belloc D71—85¢

THE BELIEF OF CATHOLICS
by Ronald Knox D72—75¢

FAITH AND FREEDOM
by Barbara Ward D73—95¢

GOD AND INTELLIGENCE IN
MODERN PHILOSOPHY
by Fulton J. Sheen D74—$1.25

If your bookseller is unable to supply certain titles, write to Image
Books, Department MIB, Garden City, New York, stating the
titles you desire and enclosing the price of each book (plus 5¢
per book to cover cost of postage and handling). Prices are subject to change without notice.

Image Books

... MAKING THE WORLD'S FINEST CATHOLIC LITERATURE AVAILABLE TO ALL

THE IDEA OF A UNIVERSITY
By John Henry Cardinal Newman. Introduction by George N. Shuster   D75—$1.45

PLAYED BY EAR: *The Autobiography of Father Daniel A. Lord, S.J.*   D76—95¢

MY BELOVED: *The Story of a Carmelite Nun.* By Mother Catherine Thomas   D77—75¢

DARK NIGHT OF THE SOUL
By St. John of the Cross. Edited and translated by E. Allison Peers   D78—75¢

TERESA OF AVILA
By Marcelle Auclair. Translated by Kathleen Pond   D79—$1.45

SAINT PETER THE APOSTLE
By William Thomas Walsh   D80—95¢

THE LOVE OF GOD
By Dom Aelred Graham, O.S.B.   D81—85¢

WOMAN OF THE PHARISEES
By François Mauriac. Translated by Gerard Hopkins   D82—75¢

THE PILLAR OF FIRE
By Karl Stern   D83—85¢

ORTHODOXY
By G. K. Chesterton   D84—75¢

THIS IS CATHOLICISM
By John J. Walsh   D85—$1.25

MEDIEVAL ESSAYS
By Christopher Dawson   D86—95¢

VESSEL OF CLAY
By Leo Trese   D87—65¢

SAINTS FOR SINNERS
By Alban Goodier, S.J.   D88—75¢

THE LONG LONELINESS
By Dorothy Day   D89—85¢

THIS IS THE MASS
By Henri Daniel-Rops. Photographs of Bishop Fulton J. Sheen by Karsh   D90—95¢

THE ORIGIN OF THE JESUITS
By James Brodrick, S.J.   D91—85¢

A POPULAR HISTORY OF THE REFORMATION
By Philip Hughes   D92—95¢

THE RESTLESS FLAME
By Louis de Wohl   D93—85¢

PROGRESS AND RELIGION
By Christopher Dawson   D94—85¢

THE CATHOLIC CHURCH IN THE MODERN WORLD
By E. E. Y. Hales   D95—95¢

THE LIFE OF TERESA OF JESUS: *The Autobiography of St. Teresa of Avila.* Translated and with an introduction by E. Allison Peers   D96—$1.25

GIANTS OF THE FAITH
By John A. O'Brien   D97—95¢

SCHOLASTICISM AND POLITICS
By Jacques Maritain   D98—95¢

THE SON OF GOD
By Karl Adam   D99—85¢

THE MAN WHO WAS CHESTERTON
Edited by Raymond T. Bond   D100—$1.45

Image Books

... MAKING THE WORLD'S FINEST CATHOLIC LITERATURE AVAILABLE TO ALL

THE CONFESSIONS OF ST. AUGUSTINE
Translated, with an introduction and notes, by John K. Ryan
D101—$1.35

HEART IN PILGRIMAGE
By Evelyn Eaton and Edward Roberts Moore D102—75¢

THE HEART OF MAN
By Gerald Vann, O.P. D103—75¢

BABY GROWS IN AGE AND GRACE
By Sister Mary de Lourdes D104—75¢

ESSAY ON THE DEVELOPMENT OF CHRISTIAN DOCTRINE
By John Henry Cardinal Newman
Introduction by Gustave Weigel, S.J.
D105—$1.35

THE STORY OF AMERICAN CATHOLICISM, 2 Volumes
By Theodore Maynard
D106A—95¢
D106B—95¢

THE CASE OF CORNELIA CONNELLY
By Juliana Wadham D107—85¢

UNDERSTANDING EUROPE
By Christopher Dawson
D108—95¢

THE DIVINE PITY
By Gerald Vann, O.P. D109—75¢

SPIRITUAL CANTICLE
By St. John of the Cross
Translated, with an introduction and notes, by E. Allison Peers
D110—$1.45

THE WHITE FATHERS
By Glenn D. Kittler D111—95¢

SAINT AMONG SAVAGES:
The Life of Isaac Jogues
By Francis Talbot, S.J.
D112—$1.45

THE THIRD REVOLUTION:
A Study of Psychiatry and Religion
By Karl Stern D113—75¢

WE HAVE BEEN FRIENDS TOGETHER and ADVENTURES IN GRACE
By Raissa Maritain D114—$1.25

WE DIE STANDING UP
Dom Hubert van Zeller, O.S.B.
D115—65¢

STAGE OF FOOLS:
A Novel of Sir Thomas More
By Charles A. Brady D116—95¢

THIS IS ROME:
A Pilgrimage in Words and Pictures
Conducted by Fulton J. Sheen
Described by H. V. Morton
Photographed by Yousuf Karsh
D117—95¢

A WOMAN CLOTHED WITH THE SUN
Edited by John J. Delaney
D118—85¢

ST. AUGUSTINE OF HIPPO
By Hugh Pope, O.P. D119—$1.35

INTERIOR CASTLE
By St. Teresa of Avila
Translated, with an introduction and notes, by E. Allison Peers
D120—75¢

THE GREATEST STORY EVER TOLD
By Fulton Oursler D121—95¢

THE MEANING OF MAN
By Jean Mouroux D122—85¢

WE AND OUR CHILDREN
By Mary Reed Newland D123—85¢

SOUL OF THE APOSTOLATE
By Jean-Baptiste Chautard, O.C.S.O. D124—85¢

CATHOLIC VIEWPOINT ON CENSORSHIP
By Harold C. Gardiner, S.J.
D125—75¢

THE SONG AT THE SCAFFOLD
By Gertrud von Le Fort D126—65¢

Image Books

. . . making the world's finest Catholic literature available to all

A HISTORY OF PHILOSOPHY, Vol. 3:

Late Mediaeval and Renaissance Philosophy, Parts I & II
By Frederick Copleston, S.J.

A magnificent exposition of philosophical thought from Ockham to the Speculative Mystics (Part I), and from the Revival of Platonism to Suarez (Part II).
D136A & D136B—95¢ ea. vol.

CATHOLIC VIEWPOINT ON EDUCATION

By Neil McCluskey, S.J.

A complete, authoritative, and clear-cut presentation of the Catholic viewpoint on a vitally urgent national issue. "Required reading"—*N.Y. Times*.
D149—75¢

MIRACLE AT CARVILLE

By Betty Martin

The story of a courageous girl's triumph over the world's most feared malady. D150—85¢

CATHEDRAL AND CRUSADE (2 volumes)

By Henri Daniel-Rops

A history of the stirring age between the eleventh and fourteenth centuries. "An important work of Catholic scholarship."—*The Saturday Review*.
D154A & D154B—$1.35 ea. vol.

SEARCHING THE SCRIPTURES

By John J. Dougherty

A popular and lucid guide to the reading and study of the Bible, giving historical background and theological explanations. D151—75¢

TRANSFORMATION IN CHRIST

By Dietrich von Hildebrand

Presents a profound analysis of the Christian experience and offers a rich new insight into the reality of the Christian life.
D152—$1.35

SECRETS OF THE SAINTS

By Henri Gheon

Four complete biographies in one volume: the Curé of Ars, the Little Flower, St. Margaret Mary, and St. John Bosco.
D153—$1.25

A DOCTOR AT CALVARY

By Pierre Barbet, M.D.

The classic and moving account of the Passion of Our Lord as described by a physician.
D155—85¢

MARY IN OUR LIFE

By William G. Most

A comprehensive and beautifully written study of Mary's importance in one's faith. D156—95¢

Image Books

*. . . making the world's finest
Catholic literature available to all*

ON THE LOVE OF GOD
(2 volumes)
*by St. Francis de Sales
Trans., with an Introduction by
John K. Ryan*

The great spiritual classic—often
called a companion volume to
Introduction to the Devout Life
—in a distinguished new translation.

D164A & 164B   95¢ ea. vol.

THE SANDS OF TAMANRASSET
by Marion Mill Preminger

The exciting story of Charles
de Foucauld—playboy, soldier,
aristocrat—who became a true
hero of God.   **D160   85¢**

**BLITHE SPIRITS: An Anthology
of Catholic Humor**
*Edited by Dan Herr and Joel
Wells*

A sparkling collection of witty
and humorous pieces on some
lighthearted aspects of modern
Catholic life by 25 celebrated
authors.   **D163   85¢**

A HISTORY OF PHILOSOPHY,
Volume 4
*Modern Philosophy: Descartes
to Leibniz
by Frederick Copleston, S.J.*

Another volume in the celebrated history of philosophy described by Blackfriars as "the
standard history of philosophy
for many years to come."

D137 $1.35

WE LIVE WITH OUR EYES OPEN
*by Dom Hubert van Zeller,
O.S.B.*

Stimulating and rewarding meditations on the spiritual life for
today's lay men and women.

D162   75¢

THE PROTESTANT REFORMATION
(2 volumes)
by Henri Daniel-Rops

"An excellent and moving syn-
thesis of one of the most critical
periods in the history of the
Church."—*The Sign*

D159A & 159B $1.35 ea. vol.

**YOUR CHILD'S WORLD: From In-
fancy through Adolescence**
by Robert Odenwald, M.D.

A new handbook of practical
advice and guidance by a leading Catholic psychiatrist.

D161   75¢

THE BOOK OF MARY
by Henri Daniel-Rops

An absorbing account of the
life and times of "the most ap-
pealing of all figures in the
Gospels," the Mother of God.

D158   75¢

PRAYER IN PRACTICE
by Romano Guardini

A practical and luminous introduction to prayer by an eminent theologian.   **D157   75¢**

I 34

Image Books

*. . . making the world's finest
Catholic literature available to all*

**A HISTORY OF PHILOSOPHY:
MODERN PHILOSOPHY, Vol. 5**
*The British Philosophers,
Hobbes to Hume (Parts I & II)
by Frederick Copleston, S.J.*
Covers the whole scope of British philosophy during the seventeenth and eighteenth centuries.

D138A & D138B 95¢ ea. vol.

LIFE OF ST. DOMINIC
by Bede Jarrett, O.P.
Outstanding biography of the founder of the Dominican Order. D165 75¢

IN SOFT GARMENTS
by Ronald Knox
Treats the challenges and problems which face today's Catholics in a sympathetic, skillful, and witty manner. D166 75¢

**THE YEAR AND OUR CHILDREN:
Planning the Family Activities
for the Church Year**
by Mary Reed Newland
A handbook showing how to initiate children into the true spirit of the Church year.
D167 95¢

**THE CHURCH IN CRISIS: A
History of the General Councils,
325–1870**
by Philip Hughes
A comprehensive survey of the origins, accomplishments, and significance of the Councils through 1500 years of history.
D168 $1.25

**ISRAEL AND THE ANCIENT
WORLD**
by Henri Daniel-Rops
A history of the Israelites from the time of Abraham to the birth of Christ. D169 $1.35

**THE SPIRITUAL EXERCISES OF
ST. IGNATIUS**
*Trans. by Anthony Mottola,
Ph.D. Intro. by Robert W. Gleason, S.J.*
A new translation of St. Ignatius' profound classic of spirituality. D170 85¢

**A NEWMAN READER: An
Anthology of the Writings of
John Henry Cardinal Newman**
*Edited, with Introduction, by
Francis X. Connolly*
A collection of the works of Newman encompassing the full range of his remarkable intellectual achievements.
D171 $1.45

WITH LOVE AND LAUGHTER
by Sister Maryanna, O.P.
A rainbow of memories in the life of an American girl who became a Dominican Sister.
D172 95¢

THE GOLDEN STRING
by Bede Griffiths, O.S.B.
The inspiring autobiography of a man's intense search for God.
D173 75¢

If your bookseller is unable to supply certain titles, write to Image Books, Department MIB, Garden City, New York, stating the titles you desire and enclosing the price of each book (plus 5¢ per book to cover cost of postage and handling). Prices are subject to change without notice.

Image Books

*. . . making the world's finest
Catholic literature available to all*

**A HISTORY OF PHILOSOPHY:
MODERN PHILOSOPHY**
Volume 6 (Parts I & II)
by Frederick Copleston, S.J.
Covers the entire scope of
18th-century Continental philosophers from The French Enlightenment to Kant.

D139A & D139B—95¢ ea. vol.

THESE ARE THE SACRAMENTS
Described by Fulton J. Sheen
Photographed by Yousuf Karsh
A clearly explained and vividly
illustrated presentation of the
seven sacraments of the Catholic
Church.   D174—95¢

**FRANCIS: A Biography of the Saint
of Assisi**
by Michael de la Bedoyere
A remarkable job of capturing
the human qualities of Francis
and revealing him as a saint for
modern times.   D175—85¢

THE WAY OF PERFECTION
by St. Teresa of Avila
Translated & edited by E. Allison Peers
The superb spiritual classic dealing with the life of prayer.
              D176—85¢

REFLECTIONS ON AMERICA
by Jacques Maritain
Sympathetic and illuminating
reflections on contemporary
American life and culture.
              D177—75¢

THE HIDDEN STREAM
by Ronald Knox
Stimulating discussions of some
fundamental precepts of the
Catholic faith.   D178—75¢

THE CATHOLIC REFORMATION
(2 volumes)
by Henri Daniel-Rops
The fifth volume of the comprehensive survey-study of the
Church dealing specifically with
the period from 1500 to 1622.

D179A & D179B—$1.25 ea. vol.

**WE SING WHILE THERE'S VOICE
LEFT**
*by Dom Hubert van Zeller,
O.S.B.*
A series of meditations on the
ways and means of attaining
spiritual perfection in our challenging times.   D180—75¢

WE HOLD THESE TRUTHS:
Catholic Reflections on the
American Proposition
by John Courtney Murray, S.J.
"Probably the most significant
Roman Catholic statement on
American democracy ever published." *New York Times Book
Review*   D181—$1.25

LETTERS FROM VATICAN CITY
by Xavier Rynne
A fascinating description of the
events and personalities of the
first session of the Ecumenical
Council. ". . . a remarkably
comprehensive and lucid study
of a very complicated subject."
Atlantic Monthly   D182—95¢

LIFE AND HOLINESS
by Thomas Merton
". . . a powerful, simple and
beautiful exposition of the principles of the spiritual life."
Jubilee   D183—75¢

If your bookseller is unable to supply certain titles, write to Image
Books, Department MIB, Garden City, New York, stating the titles
you desire and enclosing the price of each book (plus 5¢ per book
to cover cost of postage and handling). Prices are subject to change
without notice.   I 36

Image Books

. . . making the world's finest
Catholic literature available to all

A MAN NAMED JOHN: The Life of Pope John XXIII
by Alden Hatch
The complete biography of Pope John XXIII, written in a style that is fluent, warm, and popular. D184—95¢

MY LIFE WITH CHRIST
by Anthony J. Paone, S.J.
A basic book of spiritual meditations drawn from the life of Christ and aimed at the modern man caught up in the turmoil of contemporary society.
D185—95¢

THE EMERGING LAYMAN: The Role of the Catholic Layman in America
by Donald J. Thorman
An examination of the present status of the American Catholic layman and his relationship to his God, his family, his community and the world. "A book to be read and reread, to be underscored and annotated . . ."
—*The Critic* D186—85¢

A FAMILY ON WHEELS: Further Adventures of the Trapp Family Singers
by Maria Augusta Trapp with Ruth T. Murdoch
The enchanting story of the highly successful American and international concert tours of the Trapp family singers—the group upon which Richard Rodgers based his musical hit, *The Sound of Music.*
D187—75¢

THE SOCIAL AND POLITICAL PHILOSOPHY OF JACQUES MARITAIN Selected Readings
Ed. by Joseph W. Evans & Leo R. Ward
A valuable one-volume collection of Professor Maritain's writings that are both representative and expressive of his social and political philosophy.
D188—$1.45

THE FIRST JESUIT: A Biography of St. Ignatius Loyola
by Mary Purcell
Foreword by John LaFarge, S.J.
A remarkably comprehensive biography of a great man and a human saint stressing above all the human side of the man.
D189—$1.35

AMERICAN CATHOLICISM
by John Tracy Ellis
A comprehensive survey of the history of the Catholic Church in America from the days of the first Spanish and French missionaries down to the present time. D190—85¢

THE CHURCH IN THE SEVENTEENTH CENTURY (2 vols.)
by Henri Daniel-Rops
The sixth portion of Henri Daniel-Rops' monumental *The History of the Church of Christ.* These two volumes re-create a fascinating era in the history of the Western world.
D191A & D191B—$1.25 ea. vol.

If your bookseller is unable to supply certain titles, write to Image Books, Department MIB, Garden City, New York, stating the titles you desire and enclosing the price of each book (plus 5¢ per book to cover cost of postage and handling). Prices are subject to change without notice.